PHILADELPHIA

A WALK THROUGH HISTORY

Natalie Pompilio

Reedy Press
PO Box 5131
St. Louis, MO 63139
reedypress.com

Front cover inset photos (l to r):
Mural by Willis Nomo Humphrey courtesy the South Street Headhouse District via Visit Philadelphia, Walnut Street Prison courtesy the Athenaeum of Philadelphia, Mother Bethel African Methodist Church courtesy P. Meyer for Visit Philadelphia, London Coffee House courtesy Free Library of Pennysylvania, Congress Hall courtesy M. Edlow for Visit Philadelphia

Back cover inset photos:
(Top left) National Liberty Museum courtesy National Liberty Museum, (top right) Liberty Bell Center courtesy J. S. Ruth for Visit Philadelphia, (bottom) Independence Hall courtesy Visit Philadelphia

Cover photo courtesy of Tricia Pompilio (triciapompiliophotography.com)

All images are courtesy of the author unless otherwise noted.

ISBN: 9781681066103

Printed in the United States

25 26 27 28 29 5 4 3 2 1

Table of Contents

Foreword

Philadelphia is one of the nation's most walkable cities. This guide focuses on its historic core, including America's Most Historic Square Mile, making it perfect for visitors, especially those in town celebrating the nation's 250th anniversary celebration in 2026.

Like many early settlements, Philadelphia grew around its primary river, the Delaware, and was the region's busiest port in colonial times and during the nation's early years. Signs of those times remain: narrow streets unpassable by cars, homes built tall and narrow to conserve land, and cobblestone roads never paved.

I've lived in Philadelphia for more than 20 years, and I walk almost everywhere. I live on an alley off another alley. I have a brick sidewalk in front of my row house, which is connected to my neighbors on each side. If I decide to walk the six blocks to my sister's home, I'll pass Settlement Music School, a 125-plus-year-old community offering with alumni including Albert Einstein, and the Sparks Shot Tower, used to make ammunition during the Civil War. If I walk three blocks in the other direction, I can see a historic Italian American church and Mario Lanza's birthplace before reaching the country's longest continuously operated outdoor market. (That's the Italian Market, also known as the South 9th Street Market.) If, after stocking up on fresh fruit and vegetables, I take a different route home, I'll stroll through Little Saigon, a newer neighborhood. The Liberty Bell is less than a mile away.

Since most of us learned a lot about American history in school, I tried to include little-known facts about some historic places and figures. Did you know that the Founding Fathers were harassed by horseflies as they signed the Declaration of Independence? Or that nine of those signers died fighting in the Revolutionary War? Can you imagine George Washington walking from the original President's House to Washington Square, where thousands of soldiers who'd served him were buried?

The walks offered here are limited geographically, but Philadelphia has so much more to explore. Other walking tour websites or books can help visitors expand their exploration, including three of my own: *More Philadelphia Murals and the Stories They Tell* (Temple University Press, 2005); *Walking Philadelphia: 30 Walking Tours Exploring Art, Architecture, History, and Little-Known Gems* (Wilderness Press, 2nd edition 2022); and *This Used to Be Philadelphia* (Reedy Press, 2021).

Introduction

US history begins in Philadelphia. The decision to break with Britain was made by ordinary men who knew they were risking their lives when they signed the Declaration of Independence and sent it to King George III. These oft-lauded "Founding Fathers" walked these streets and visited these buildings. They were real people who complained about the summer heat, drank to excess, had friends and enemies, and had no idea if the steps they were taking were the right ones.

Before the Constitution was written and ratified, citizens weren't sure how their chosen leaders would structure their government. They'd just survived an almost eight-year-long war they'd entered outmanned and outgunned. George Washington was a national hero, and some suggested he be made king.

Washington, however, nixed that idea. Instead, he served as presiding officer of the Constitutional Convention, the gathering during which representatives from the 13 colonies debated how best to govern. When it was decided, a passerby stopped Franklin as he left the meeting and asked, "What have we got, a republic or a monarchy?" His famous answer: "A republic, if you can keep it."

As the nation celebrates the 250th anniversary of the signing of the Declaration of Independence, people are once again questioning how the country should be run. Knowing our history is more important than ever.

These walks are sorted by theme. Some sites appear in more than one walk. Independence Hall, for example, is included in four tours, but each entry contains different information. Most of the walks are a mile or less.

Philadelphia is one of the nation's most walkable cities, with a downtown grid introduced by William Penn in 1682. In 2024, *USA Today*'s editors and readers ranked it the country's "Most Walkable City to Visit." (It got the same nod in 2023.) Philly's also the nation's first UNESCO World Heritage site, home to almost 70 national landmarks.

While these walks are centered on history, modern Philadelphia has a lot to offer as well. With 1.6 million residents spread across 135 square miles, it doesn't have Manhattan's crowding or Washington, DC's, sterile feel. There's something for everyone: fine dining restaurants and food courts, high-end retail chains and unique boutiques. For sports lovers, the city has winning franchises in every major category, including the Philadelphia Eagles, winners of 2025's Super Bowl LIX. Our museums, including the National Constitutional Center and the Museum of the American Revolution, are among the nation's finest.

Old easily mixes with new here: On one block in the Society Hill neighborhood, electric car chargers sit next to traditional horse-hitching posts. Historic reenactors in costume walk next to suited business people and students in uniforms. It's fun to see a Benjamin Franklin sending a text message or a Betsy Ross riding in a car moving slowly behind a horse-drawn carriage. Streets with names derived from the native Lenni-Lenape language—including Passyunk (in the valley) Avenue and Moyamensing (the place of pigeon droppings) Street—aren't far from Interstate 95.

Welcome to Philadelphia.

Happy Semiquincentennial!

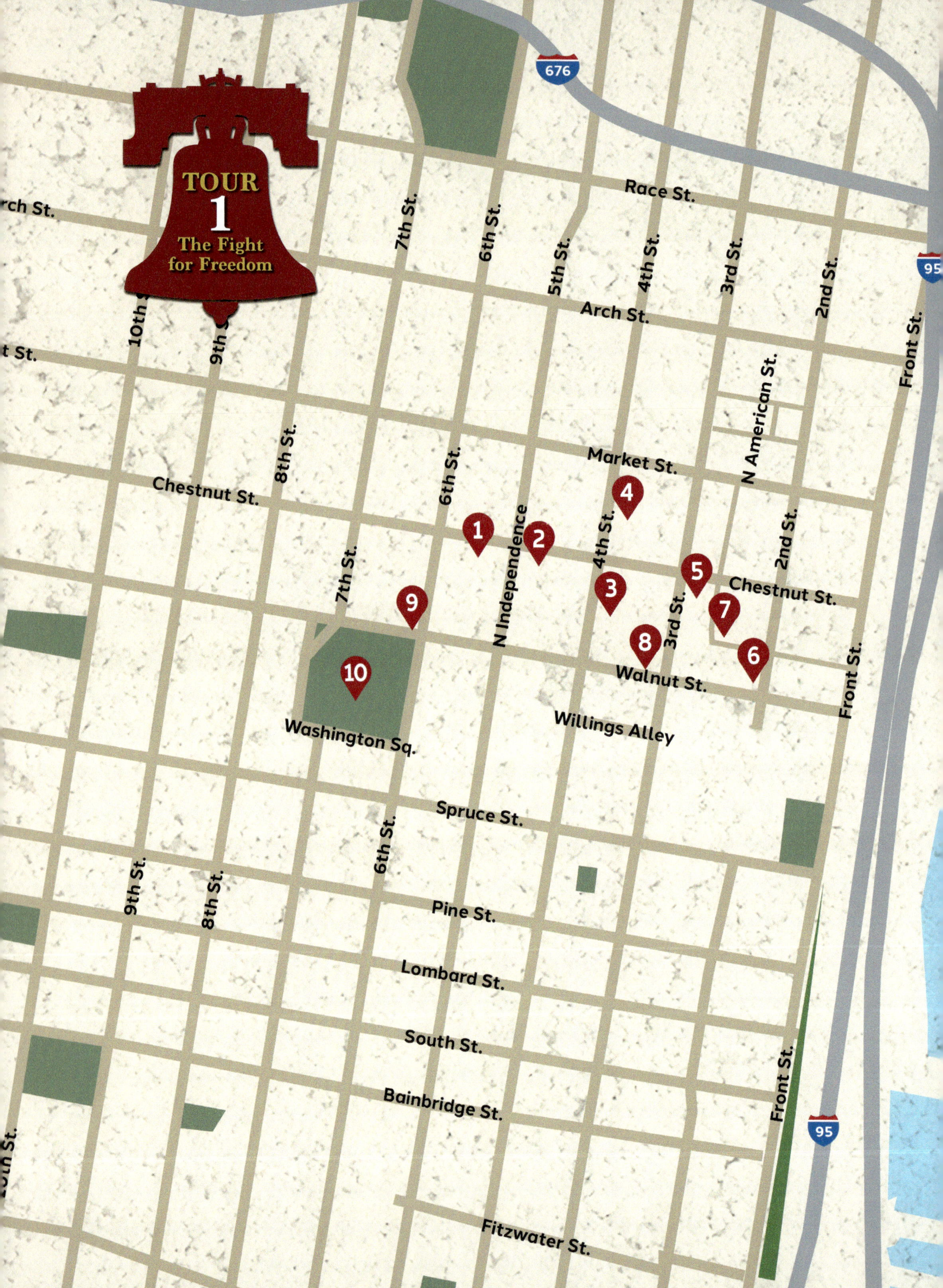
TOUR
1
The Fight for Freedom
676
95
Race St.
Arch St.
Market St.
Chestnut St.
Walnut St.
Willings Alley
Washington Sq.
Spruce St.
Pine St.
Lombard St.
South St.
Bainbridge St.
Fitzwater St.
10th St.
9th St.
8th St.
7th St.
6th St.
5th St.
N Independence
4th St.
3rd St.
N American St.
2nd St.
Front St.
1
2
3
4
5
6
7
8
9
10

TOUR 1

THE FIGHT FOR FREEDOM–The Declaration of Independence

In July 1776, when 56 citizens affixed their names to a document declaring Great Britain's 13 North American colonies independent of the king, they were committing a treasonous act punishable by death. While some of these men, now known as the Founding Fathers, were wealthy and influential individuals, others were farmers or merchants. Benjamin Franklin said at the signing, "We must, indeed, all hang together, or, most assuredly, we shall all hang separately."

One delegate described the atmosphere on the day of the signing as a "pensive and awful silence which pervaded the house when we were called up, one after another, to the table of the President of Congress to subscribe what was believed by many at that time to be our own death warrants."

Begin at Independence Hall, South 6th and Chestnut Streets.

1 Independence Hall
S 6th and Chestnut Sts.

◆ The hall was built as the Pennsylvania State House in the mid-1700s. In 1775, the Second Continental Congress convened here to debate breaking with British rule. It's called "the birthplace of America" because the country's two founding documents—the Declaration of Independence and the Constitution—were signed and ratified here.

July 1776 was excessively hot and muggy. When it was time to sign the Declaration, someone opened an Independence Hall window to allow a draft into the room. Insects followed. As one Thomas Jefferson biographer wrote, the biting flies "assailed the silk-stockinged legs of honorable members. Handkerchief in hand, they lashed the flies with such vigor that they could command on a July afternoon; but the annoyance became at length so extreme as to render them impatient of delay. . . ."

Front view of Independence Hall on Chestnut Street facing Independence Mall. Courtesy of Visit Philadelphia

Walk one block east.

2 Signers Garden
5th and Chestnut

◆ Signers (alternately written as Signer's and Signers') Garden honors the signers of the Declaration of Independence. The center statue depicts Philadelphian George Clymer, his left arm raised and a rolled-up copy of the Declaration in his hand. Clymer is one of only six men who signed both the Declaration of Independence and the US Constitution. A merchant by trade, Clymer was an early advocate for making a complete break with

Philadelphia merchant George Clymer holds up a copy of the Declaration of Independence. Courtesy of the National Park Service

England and took part in public demonstrations protesting the Stamp Act and the Tea Act. He was elected to the first US Congress in 1789.

Close your eyes briefly, then reopen to look on the same space. Imagine not a garden but a three-story brick home.

The image of Washington on the $1 bill was based on this unfinished portrait by Gilbert Stuart.

◆ On this spot once stood **Gilbert Stuart House**, the residence and workplace of the artist who painted more than 1,000 portraits of well-known politicians, world leaders, and high-society members, including the first six US presidents, France's King Louis XVI, and England's King George III. Stuart's most famous work is *Athenaeum Head*. Not ringing a (liberty) bell? It's the oil painting of George Washington used to create the engraving on the dollar bill. Washington was in his mid-60s when he sat for this painting. Stuart later noted that, "When I painted [Washington], he had just had a set of false teeth inserted, which accounts for the constrained expression so noticeable about the mouth and the lower part of the face."

Continue walking east on Chestnut for two blocks.

This painting of the First Continental Congress in front of Carpenters Hall was painted in 1911. Courtesy of Philadelphia History Museum at Atwater Kent

3 Carpenters Hall
320 Chestnut St.

◆ This building hosted the First Continental Congress in September 1774, which drew up a list of desired rights and perceived grievances against the British monarchy but accomplished little else. During debate, Patrick Henry famously stood and said, "The distinctions between Virginians, Pennsylvanians, New Yorkers, and New Englanders are no more. I am not a Virginian but an American." An inscription over the building's south hall reads "Within these Walls Henry, Hancock, & Adams inspired the Delegates of the Colonies with Verve and Sinew for the Toils of War."

Continue east.

This steel "ghost structure" is the outline of the home where Ben Franklin lived until his death in 1790. Courtesy of the National Park Service

The Museum of the American Revolution features George Washington's war tent. Courtesy of J. Fusco for Visit Philadelphia

4 Benjamin Franklin Museum and Franklin Court

317 Chestnut St. (The property is a block wide and has an entrance on Walnut St.)

❖ Benjamin Franklin's accomplishments are too numerous to list. He seemed to have a hand in everything: He was postmaster, newspaper writer and owner, insurance-company founder, university builder, and electricity-seeking madman, among other things. In 1774, Franklin published the famous "Join or Die" cartoon in a Philadelphia newspaper that he owned. The political cartoon shows a snake cut into pieces, with each piece labeled with the name of a colony. The message: The colonies needed to come together to fight the outside forces opposing them.

Thomas Jefferson asked Franklin to edit the Declaration, writing: "Will Doctr. Franklin be so good to peruse it and suggest such alterations as his more enlarged view of the subject will dictate?"

Continue east.

5 Museum of the American Revolution

101 S 3rd St.

❖ Soon after the Museum of the American Revolution opened in 2017, a group of schoolchildren hopped up on *Hamilton* ran from exhibit to exhibit, singing songs from the Broadway show. The museum highlights military leaders and the battles they fought as well as the ordinary people who became revolutionaries. One highlight is Washington's War Tent, the fabric that sheltered the Continental Army general from the elements on the battlefield. Also on exhibit: one of Washington's 13-starred headquarters flags, a mug from the 1770s that still smells like rum, a pair of baby booties made from a British army officer's jacket, and a calfskin wallet made from a Revolutionary War drumhead.

Continue east, turning right onto South 2nd Street.

6 City Tavern

138 S 2nd St.

❖ The building is a reproduction of the original 1773 structure. The Founding Fathers kept this pub busy while hammering out the details of the Declaration of Independence and the Constitution, eating and sleeping here. The tavern's booths and private rooms made private conversations easier. During the Second Continental Congress, delegates including John Adams and Benjamin Franklin ate here daily. Jefferson had an open account. As UShistory.org describes it, "The tavern was considered the finest establishment of its time in

The Founding Fathers ate at City Tavern while hammering out details to the Declaration of Independence and the Constitution. Courtesy of the National Park Service

the colonies. In one room, a patron might hear a concert or an opera; in another, the latest political news; in yet another the price of sows and sorghum."

Continue walking south to Walnut Street, then turn right.

7 The Portrait Gallery

143 S 3rd St. (in the Second Bank of the United States)

❖ This museum offers *People of Independence*, a permanent exhibit that includes more than 150 portraits of politicians, military leaders, and well-known citizens. More than 100 of them are the work of famed artist Charles Willson Peale. Peale served as a captain in the Continental Army, fighting at the Battles of Trenton and Princeton. Sitting for portraits was trying, as John Adams, the second president of the United States, noted: "Speaking generally, no penance is like having one's picture done. You must sit in a constrained and unnatural position, which is a trial to the temper."

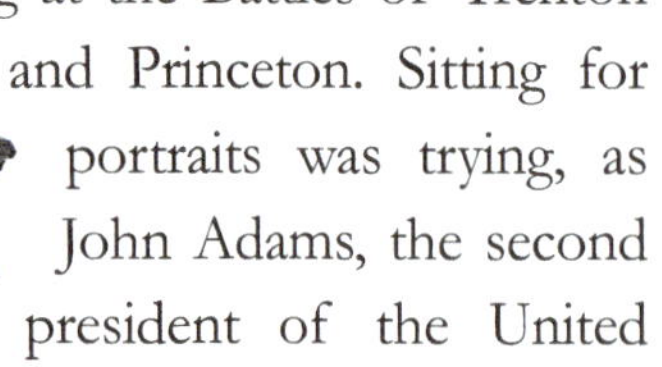

Of the 150 portraits in the Portrait Gallery of the Second Bank of the US, more than 100 are by Charles Willson Peale. Courtesy of the National Park Service

Continue west on Walnut Street.

8 Bishop William White House

309 Walnut St.

❖ The Right Reverend William White, rector at two of the founders' favorite churches, lived here until he died in his third-floor library in 1836. George Washington was a close friend, and Benjamin Rush, who signed the Declaration and ratified the Constitution, lived next door. White tended to the sick during 1793's yellow fever epidemic, which killed about 5,000 Philadelphians when the city's total population hovered around 50,000. White never became ill, leading some to say he was blessed. Others noted that White had an indoor privy, meaning he was less likely to get bitten by mosquitos when outside using an outhouse, and he often smoked a smelly cigar that likely kept away insects.

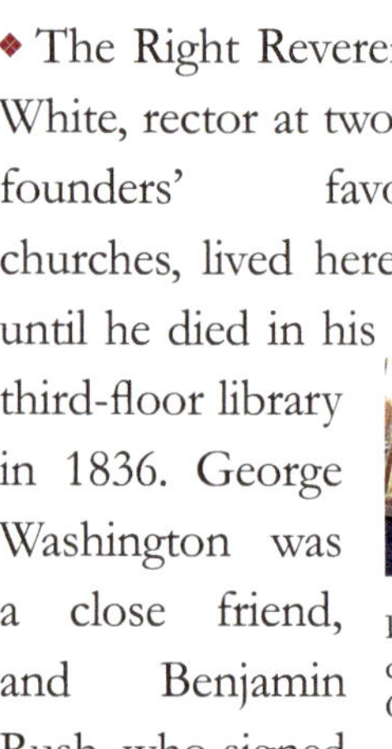

Bishop William White led services at two churches popular with the Founding Fathers. Courtesy of the National Park Service

Continue west to South 6th Street.

9 Walnut Street Prison

Walnut and S 6th Sts.

❖ Built in 1773, the facility became a debtors' prison after the war. Robert Morris, one of the richest men of his time and the so-called "Financier of the

This debtors' prison housed Robert Morris, the "financier of the American Revolution," who was never repaid. Courtesy of the Athenaeum of Philadelphia

American Revolution," was one inmate. Morris, who signed both of the nation's founding documents, is believed to have personally paid for about 80 percent of the war. (In 2010, the Congressional Research Service estimated the war's cost in modern dollars at $2.4 billion.) Morris never asked to be reimbursed for his financial contributions. He even donated his home to President George Washington to use as the Executive Mansion, making it the first White House. Washington, a good friend, visited Morris during his incarceration.

Cross South 6th Street into the park.

10 Washington Square

bounded by S 6th, 7th, and Walnut Sts. and S Washington Square

❖ During the Revolutionary War, an estimated 2,000 American and British soldiers were interred here, usually in mass graves. In the 1950s, local residents decided to create a memorial for the Revolutionary War dead. Archaeologists dug up a body they believed was an American soldier—the man had a head wound consistent with a musket ball—and placed it the *Tomb of the Unknown Revolutionary War Soldier*. The memorial features a statue of George Washington and an eternal flame. One of the quotes inscribed on the tomb: "Freedom is a light for which many have died in darkness."

George Washington stands guard over the Tomb of the Revolutionary War Soldier in Washington Square. Courtesy of the National Park Service

The movie *National Treasure* implies something important is written on the back of the Declaration of Independence. The actual writing reads "Original Declaration of Independence dated 4th July 1776."

Of the 56 men who signed the Declaration of Independence, five were captured by the British and treated as traitors and nine fought and died during the Revolutionary War.

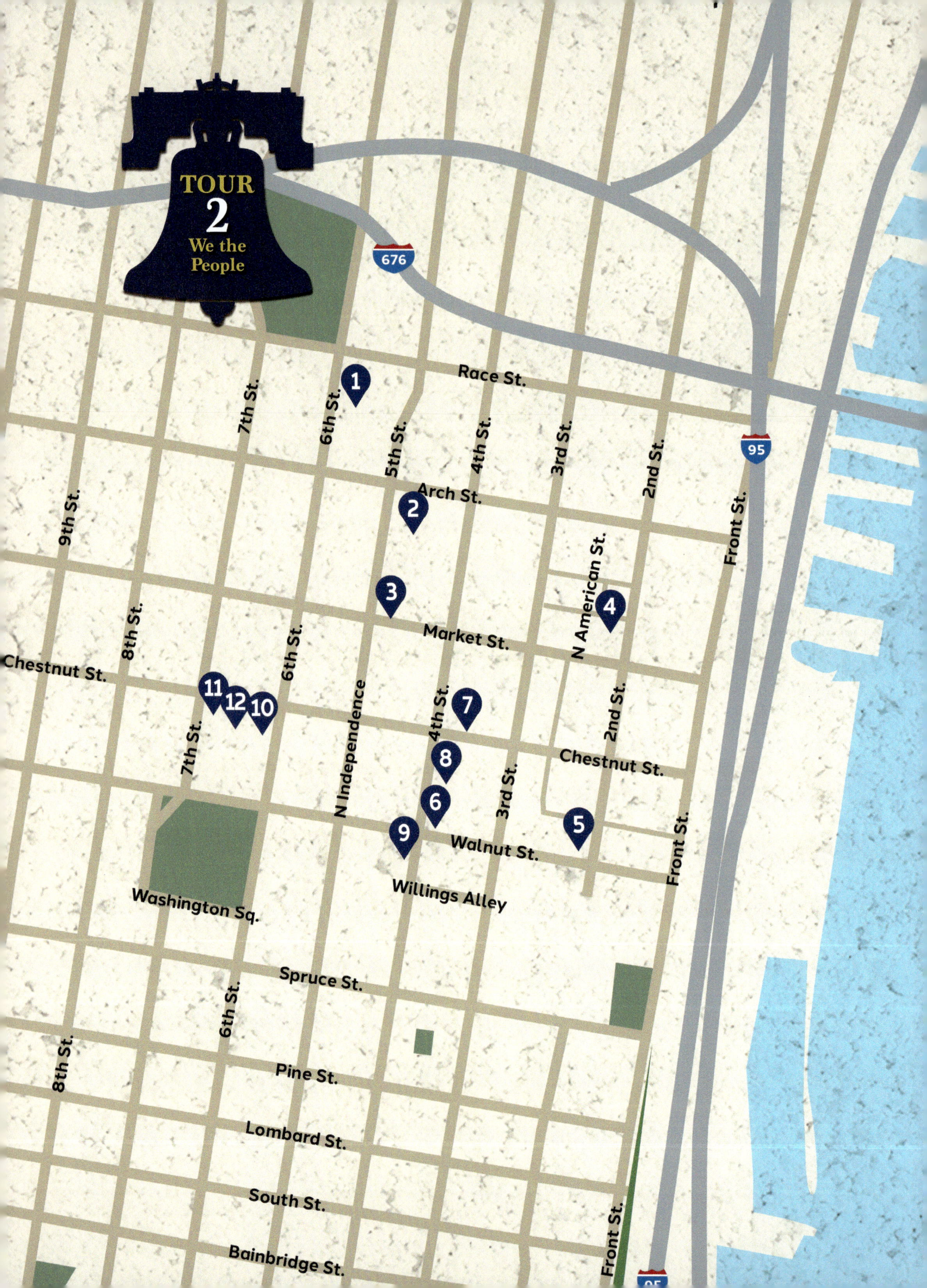

TOUR
2
We the
People
676
Race St.
1
7th St.
6th St.
5th St.
4th St.
3rd St.
2nd St.
95
Arch St.
2
9th St.
Front St.
3
N American St.
4
8th St.
Market St.
6th St.
Chestnut St.
11
12
10
N Independence
4th St.
7
7th St.
2nd St.
8
Chestnut St.
3rd St.
6
5
9
Walnut St.
Front St.
Willings Alley
Washington Sq.
Spruce St.
6th St.
8th St.
Pine St.
Lombard St.
South St.
Front St.
Bainbridge St.

TOUR 2
WE THE PEOPLE

The Constitution is the foundation of American governance, outlining the duties of its three branches and detailing the rights of its citizens. It's a living document in that people can interpret its passages differently and it can be changed as attitudes change. It has been amended 27 times. The first 10 amendments, better known as the Bill of Rights, were added in 1791. The most recent amendment, the 27th, details "Financial Compensation for the Congress," and was approved in 1992.

The National Constitution Center is the only museum devoted to the country's founding document. Courtesy of M. Kennedy for Visit Philadelphia

1 National Constitution Center
525 Arch St.

◆ This is the nation's only museum devoted to its founding document, offering interpretations of its lofty words through interactive displays, explanatory videos, and changing exhibitions. Since opening its doors on Independence Day 2003, the center has welcomed more than four million guests. The center has hosted major political debates, including the 2008 primary debate between Barack Obama and Hillary Rodham Clinton and the 2024 presidential debate between Kamala Harris and Donald Trump. The Center's Philadelphia Liberty Medal is awarded annually to individuals still actively engaged in the fight for freedom. Past honorees include world leaders, former US presidents, journalists, and individuals including Malala Yousafzai of Pakistan. One museum exhibit features life-sized statues of the Constitution's signatories, who on average stood about 5'7" tall.

 Walk south on North 5th Street.

Ben Franklin's grave in Christ Church Burial Ground was even popular in the late 1800s, when this photo was taken. Courtesy of archives.org

2 Christ Church Burial Ground
340 N 5th St.

◆ More than 4,000 Christ Church congregants rest here, including five signers of the Declaration of Independence. The cemetery's most famous grave, which can be easily seen through the fence, is that of Benjamin Franklin. It's usually littered with pennies, as it's believed that those who toss a penny on the grave will have good luck (a shout-out to Franklin's famous, "A penny saved is a penny earned").

As a young man, Franklin wrote his own epitaph: "The Body of B. Franklin, Printer/ Like the Cover of an old Book/Its Contents torn out/And stript of its Lettering and Gilding/Lies here/Food for Worms." Franklin's last words are said to have been "A dying man can do nothing easily."

 Continue south to Market Street.

3 House's Boarding House
5th and Market Sts.

◆ Three of the city's boarding houses did brisk business during the summer of 1787 as the out-of-town delegates arrived to debate the new nation's future. Mary House, a widower with two children, owned and operated these accommodations. (Yes, House is the family name.) It's unclear what the quality of Mrs. House's house was, but Thomas Jefferson had some strong feelings about the room he rented two blocks from here (Declaration House/Graff House, 7th and Market Streets). While nicely furnished and well-built, it was across the street from a horse stable. Jefferson complained to the landlords about the horseflies that attacked him. He finished the Constitution in three weeks, perhaps eager to escape the ever-present pests.

This image shows a typical boarding house on Chestnut Street circa 1859. Courtesy of the Library Company of Philadelphia (Frederick De Bourg Richards Photograph Collection)

 Turn left on Market Street. Stop at South 2nd Street.

4 Christ Church
20 N American St.

◆ Until the Covid-19 quarantine made attendance impossible, Christ Church had boasted that it had hosted a service every weekend for more than 300 years. It's the birthplace of the American Episcopal Church and sometimes called "the Nation's Church." Regular attendees included George Washington, Benjamin Franklin, and Betsy Ross.

Five signers of the Declaration of Independence attended services at Christ Church. Courtesy of P. Meyer for Visit Philadelphia

The church's bells were often rung for public events, including the signing of the Declaration of Independence. (That must have been awkward, as the church rector at the time was loyal to the British crown.) It's unclear if the bells sounded after the signing of the Constitution because they may have still been in storage outside the city: During the war, the bells of almost every city church were hidden so the British couldn't melt them for ammunition.

 Turn right onto South 2nd Street.

5 City Tavern
138 S 2nd St.

◆ City Tavern was a Founding Fathers hot spot. Thomas Jefferson praised the sweet-potato biscuits. Pepperpot stew, which Washington enjoyed after crossing the Delaware River, was a popular menu item. After agreeing on the Constitution's language, the delegates, "55 of our most

This engraving of City Tavern by William Birch depicts the building in 1800.

notable Americans," consumed "114 bottles of wine (Madeira and claret), 34 bottles of beer, eight bottles of cider, and seven large bowls of rum punch—45 gallons of booze," according to fourwallswhiskey.com. They smoked cigars and listened to a nine-piece band. They were a rowdy bunch, and the bill notes charges for broken wineglasses and other glassware. It took three days for the men to sober up enough to sign the Constitution.

 Continue south on South 2nd Street. At Walnut Street, turn right.

6 The Dolley Todd House
341 Walnut St.

◆ Before she became First Lady Dolley Madison, she was Dolley Todd, a married mother of two living in Philadelphia. After her husband died in 1793, Dolley married James Madison. (Aaron Burr was their matchmaker.) James was 43, and Dolley was 26. She became First Lady when James was elected in 1809. Before invading British soldiers burned the White House to the ground in August 1814, Dolley had servants remove Gilbert Stuart's near-life-size painting of Washington to save it "from the mockery of British soldiers," notes whitehousehistory.org. "Her respect for the portrait as a patriot symbol showed a keen sensitivity towards Americans longing for emblems that would identify their nation and bind them as a people to it."

Gilbert Stuart, whose image of George Washington is on the $1 bill, also painted this portrait of Dolley Todd Madison. Courtesy of the White House Historical Association (White House Collection)

 Return to South 2nd Street and turn around, walking north to Chestnut Street. Turn left on Chestnut Street.

7 National Liberty Museum
321 Chestnut St.

◆ Lifelong Philadelphian Irvin J. Borowsky founded this museum after his retirement "to give back to the nation by reminding people that liberty is the defining force that makes everything else that we do possible," the museum's website notes. Borowsky, who died in 2014 at age 90, was the son of Polish immigrants. He became a successful book and magazine publisher, and in 1982 he launched the American Interfaith Institute, which encouraged Jews and Christians to focus on their similarities rather than their differences. One of his projects: the publication of a Bible with a New Testament that does not blame Jews for the death of Jesus Christ.

The National Liberty Museum's goal is to remind visitors that freedom makes all that we do possible. Courtesy of the National Liberty Museum

 Continue east on Chestnut Street.

Carpenters Hall hosted the First Continental Congress in 1774. Courtesy of the National Liberty Museum

8 Carpenters Hall
320 Chestnut St.

◆ Months after the Boston Tea Party, representatives from 12 of the 13 colonies gathered here to discuss future options. (Georgia didn't send anyone.) During a seven-week span, the first Continental Congress called for a boycott of British goods and urged each colony to establish a militia. The delegates also sent a petition to King George III asking that he repeal the "Intolerable Acts"—high taxes—instituted to punish the Massachusetts Bay colony. The monarch refused, prompting all 13 colonies to send delegates to Philadelphia in 1776 for the Second Continental Congress. In 1982, the Pennsylvania legislature officially recognized this building as the birthplace of the Commonwealth of Pennsylvania.

Continue to South 4th Street.

9 The Philadelphia Contributionship
210 S 4th St.

◆ This building housed the nation's longest continuously running fire insurance company, founded by Benjamin Franklin in 1752. Policyholders were given the Contributionship's fire mark—four hands each clasping another's wrist to form a square—to prominently display outside their properties to indicate their building was insured and volunteer fire companies responding to any blaze would be paid for their work. Some of the Contributionship's coverage guidelines influenced how the city looks today: After 1769, it refused to insure wooden structures, prompting builders to use bricks.

When firefighters saw the Philadelphia Contributionship's firemark on a house, they knew they'd get paid.

Continue east on Chestnut Street. Stop at South 5th Street.

Ben Franklin and a friend started the American Philosophical Society to promote scientific experiments. Courtesy of M. Kennedy for Visit Philadelphia

10 American Philosophical Society
104 S 5th St.

◆ Benjamin Franklin and a friend established the American Philosophical Society in 1743. Its purpose: to promote advancement in all scientific fields or, as Franklin phrased it, "All philosophical Experiments that let Light into the Nature of Things, tend to increase the Power of Man over

Matter, and multiply the Conveniencies or Pleasures of Life." Members met monthly to conduct experiments. The APS built this headquarters in 1789. By 1800, the society had more than 600 elected members. Before Meriwether Lewis headed west with William Clark, he came to the APS so members could teach him how to preserve plant and animal specimens.

Continue east on Chestnut Street.

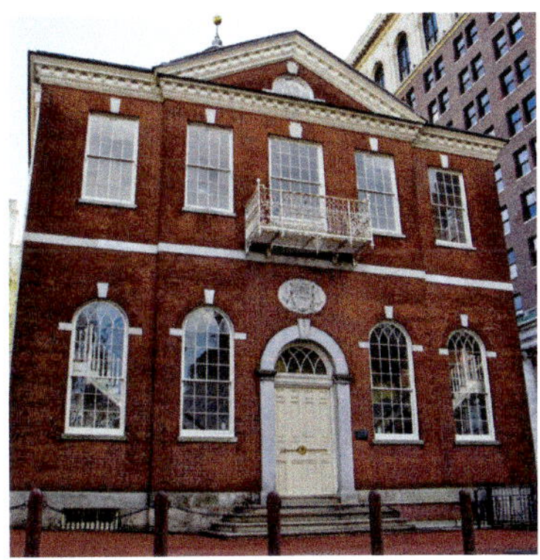

Congress Hall housed the House of Representatives on its first floor and the Senate on its second when Philadelphia was the national capital. Courtesy of M. Edlow for Visit Philadelphia

11 Congress Hall
Chestnut between S 5th and 6th Sts.

◆ For 10 years, when Philadelphia was the nation's capital, this building lived up to its name, hosting the House of Representatives on its first floor and the Senate on its second, which is how we came to refer to the Senate as the "upper chamber." George Washington took his second oath of office here. Four years later, the building saw the country's first peaceful transition of power, when Washington attended the inauguration of his replacement, John Adams. At the close of the ceremony, ushistory.org says, "John Adams waited for Washington to lead the exit, as everyone had grown accustomed to, but Washington insisted on leaving the room after the new President."

Continue east on Chestnut Street.

12 Independence Hall
S 6th and Chestnut Sts.

◆ During the Constitutional Convention of 1787, George Washington oversaw debates while sitting quietly in the "rising sun" chair, so-called because, at the convention's end, Benjamin Franklin said he'd spent three months staring at its carving "without being able to tell whether it was rising or setting. But now at length I have the happiness to know that it is a rising and not a setting sun." Washington, too, had worried about the new country's survival, writing in a 1785 letter, "We are either a united people, or we are not. If the former, let us, in all matters of general concern, act as a nation. . . . If we are not, let us no longer act a farce by pretending to it." Multiple presidents—including Abraham Lincoln and Ronald Reagan—have addressed the nation with the hall as a backdrop.

During the debate over the Constitution at Independence Hall, George Washington sat in the "rising sun" chair. Courtesy of the National Park Service

Did You Know?

The US is the world's first modern democracy, and Philadelphia is a city of American firsts. Among them: the nation's first planned city, zoo, hospital, medical school, library system, stock exchange, bank, and daily newspaper.

Philadelphia is the first UNESCO World Heritage City in the United States. Independence Hall is the city's only UNESCO World Heritage Site.

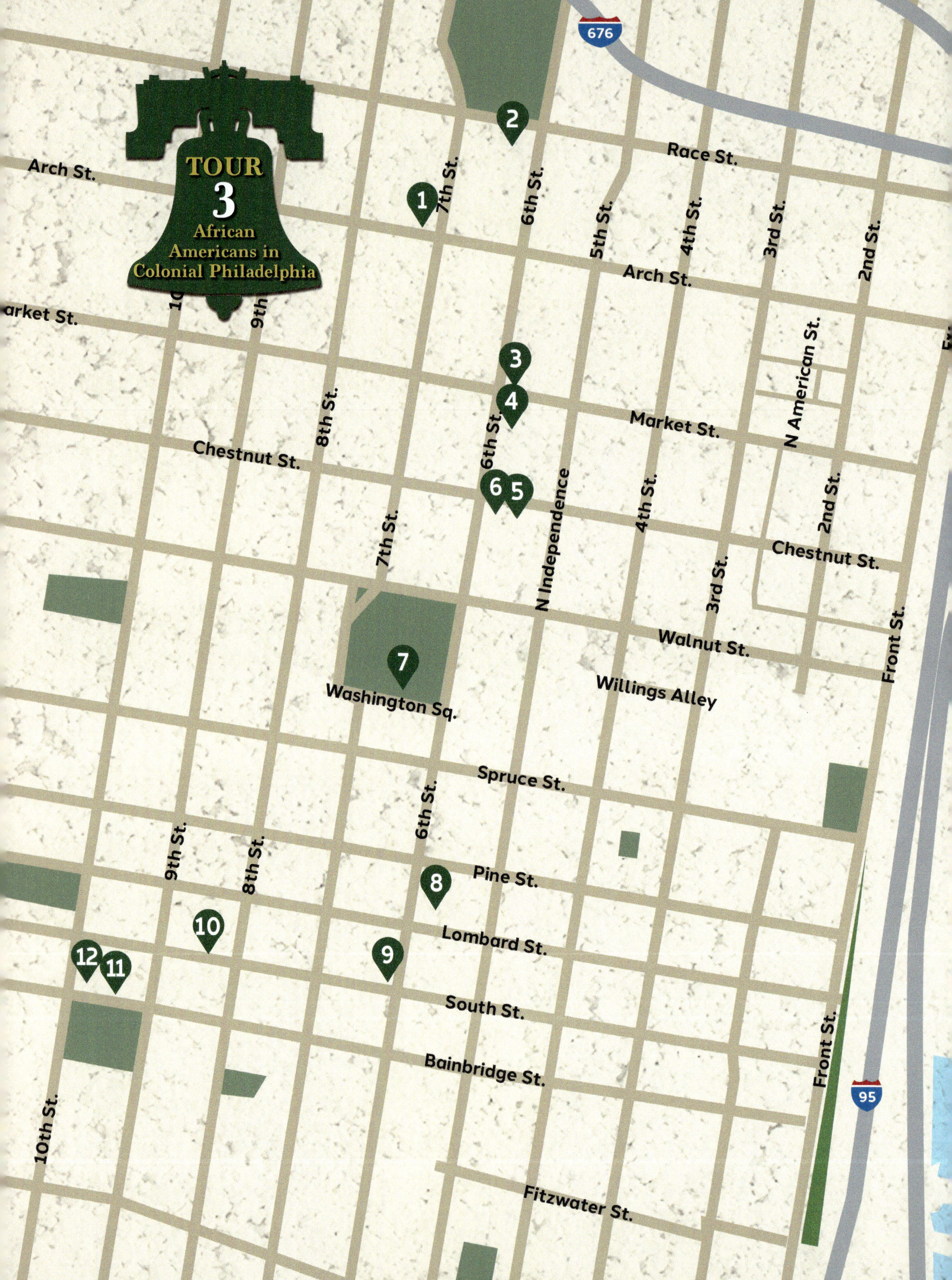
TOUR
3
African Americans in Colonial Philadelphia
676
Race St.
Arch St.
Arch St.
arket St.
Market St.
Chestnut St.
Chestnut St.
Walnut St.
Willings Alley
Washington Sq.
Spruce St.
Pine St.
Lombard St.
South St.
Bainbridge St.
Fitzwater St.
7th St.
6th St.
5th St.
4th St.
3rd St.
2nd St.
9th
8th St.
6th St.
7th St.
N Independence
4th St.
3rd St.
2nd St.
N American St.
Front St.
Front St.
9th St.
8th St.
6th St.
10th St.
95
1
2
3
4
5
6
7
8
9
10
11
12

TOUR 3
AFRICAN AMERICANS IN COLONIAL PHILADELPHIA

Enslaved Africans were first brought to Philadelphia in the 1630s by Dutch and Swiss settlers, more than four decades before William Penn arrived from England. (Despite his Quaker faith and public proclamations about the importance of individual freedoms, Penn held at least 12 enslaved people.) For the next century, the city's Delaware River port was a hub in the international trade of enslaved people.

Philadelphia was also the hub of the movement to abolish slavery. The Society for the Relief of Free Negroes Unlawfully Held in Bondage was founded here in 1775. In 1780, Pennsylvania was the first state to pass a law that would gradually end slavery by ending the import of enslaved people and declaring that all children were born free, regardless of parentage or skin color.

Begin at the corner of North 7th and Arch Streets.

1 The African American Museum
701 Arch St.

◆ The museum opened in 1976 as part of the nation's bicentennial celebration. Its permanent collection includes the works of Jack T. Franklin, a photographer who documented historic events including the 1965 Selma to Montgomery March. In front of the museum are John Rhoden's *Nesaika* and Reginald Beauchamp's *Whispering Bells: A Tribute to Crispus Attucks*. Rhoden says his work "holds the embodiment of the people who have come from the four corners of the Earth into this great now of our time." Beauchamp honors Attucks, a formerly enslaved man believed to be the first person to die in the war for independence. The 13 bells represent the 13 colonies.

The African American Museum in Philadelphia is an affiliate of the Smithsonian Institute. Courtesy of A. Ricketts for Visit Philadelphia

Walk one block east on Arch Street. Turn right at North 6th Street.

2 Pennsylvania Hall
190 N 6th St.

Abolitionist headquarters Pennsylvania Hall stood for less than a week before protesters burned it to the ground.

◆ The building belonged to the Female Anti-Slavery Society and was built in 1838 to host its annual convention. Among the more than 200 attendees was Laura Lovell of Massachusetts, who wrote in Philadelphia she believed "that I have found on earth a place where order, harmony, love and freedom prevail."

But antiabolitionists protested outside the gathering, breaking windows during speeches and hurling stones, mud, potatoes, and onions at

departing convention goers. After four days, Lovell described leaving the building to face a "mob of two or three thousand, fierce, vile looking men, and boys." Once the building was empty, these men burned it to the ground. It had stood for less than a week. It was never rebuilt.

 Continue walking south on North 6th Street, stopping at Market Street.

Alison Sky's *Indelible* can be seen on the left in this photo of Independence Visitors Center. Courtesy of A. Wendowski for Visit Philadelphia

3 Alison Sky's *Indelible*
at the Independence Visitors Center
599 Market St.

◆ The inscribed glass features text from an early version of the Declaration of Independence that was cut before the signing. Thomas Jefferson, the Declaration's main author, originally included slavery as one of King George III's crimes, writing, "He has waged cruel war against human nature itself, violating its most sacred rights of life & liberty in the persons of a distant people who never offended him, captivating & carrying them into slavery in another hemisphere, or to incur miserable death in their transportation thither . . ." Historians estimate at least one-third of the 56 signers of the Declaration of Independence enslaved people. Jefferson is believed to have enslaved more than 600 people during his lifetime.

 Cross Market Street.

This exhibit at the President's House concerns the enslaved people Washington kept here. Courtesy of J. Ellicott for the National Park Service

4 President's House
S 6th and Market Sts.

◆ In 2000, excavation work on this corner uncovered the foundations of the house where George Washington lived and worked before the nation's capital was moved to Washington, DC. The site's open-air exhibit honors the enslaved people who managed Washington's household. Pennsylvania was a free state, and any enslaved person who lived there for six months was granted freedom. To get around this, Washington sent his enslaved workers to neighboring New Jersey a few times a year. Washington considered himself a good man who took good care of the people forced into his employ and was thus mystified when two of them—Hercules, a cook, and Oney Judge, Martha Washington's personal maid—escaped.

 Continue south on South 6th Street.

5 Liberty Bell Center
S 6th and Chestnut Sts.

◆ The center houses the Liberty Bell, which was given that moniker in the 1800s when abolitionists adopted it as a symbol of their movement because of its Biblical verse inscription, *Proclaim liberty throughout all the land unto all the inhabitants thereof.* Installed in the tower of Independence Hall (then the Pennsylvania statehouse) in the mid-1700s, its

Abolitionists adopted the Liberty Bell as a symbol because of its engraving: *Proclaim Liberty throughout all the Land Unto all the inhabitants thereof.* Courtesy of J.S. Ruth for Visit Philadelphia

peals called politicians to the legislature, students to university classes, and residents to public meetings. As Ben Franklin wrote, "the Bell rings, and I must go among the Grave ones and talk Politicks." Some say the bell first cracked after its initial ringing, and that the fissure worsened after almost a century of use.

Continue south on South 6th Street, crossing Chestnut Street.

Escaped enslaved people who were recaptured had hearings at Independence Hall. Courtesy of the National Park Service

6 Independence Hall

S 6th and Chestnut Sts.

◆ Enslaved people who were recaptured were put on trial here. In 1850, lawmakers passed the Fugitive Slave Act, which allowed "slave catchers" to cross state lines in pursuit of their quarry. Of the nine cases that were heard here, seven resulted in a return to enslavement. One notable case was that of Hannah Dellem in March 1851. Hannah was in the late stages of pregnancy when she fled Maryland. If she gave birth in Pennsylvania, her child would be free. If she was forced back to Maryland and then had her baby, the child would be enslaved. The court sent her back to Maryland.

Cross South 6th Street.

7 Washington Square

◆ This park, now called Washington Square, was once dubbed Congo Square because free and enslaved African Americans often gathered here to celebrate their native countries. In the 18th century it was a graveyard for free and enslaved people as well as those who died by suicide, the poor, and victims of smallpox and yellow fever. In the mid-1700s, doctors stole bodies from the cemetery for research purposes, prompting relatives of the interred to sleep on their loved ones' graves. The cemetery was closed to burials in 1794. In the 1800s, it became an urban park. In recent years, the square has hosted Juneteenth celebrations.

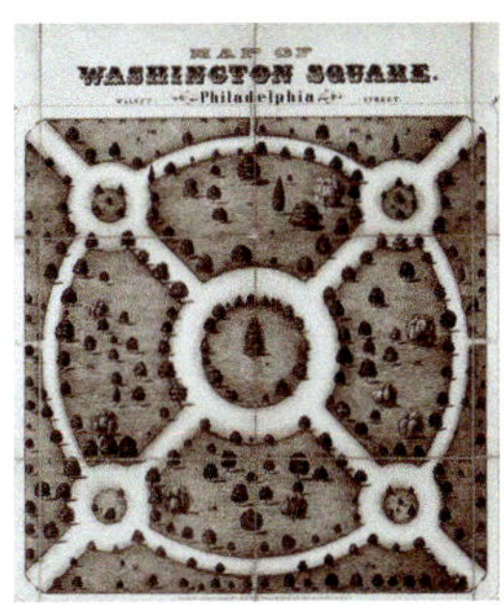

Washington Square, one of William Penn's original parks, was once called Congo Square. Courtesy of the Historical Society of Pennsylvania

8 Mother Bethel (A.M.E.) Church

419 S 6th St.

◆ This is the mother church of the country's first independent black denomination, founded in 1794 by Bishop Richard Allen. Born into slavery, Allen bought his freedom for $2,000 and completed formal studies to become a Methodist minister. Beneath the church is a mile-long underground tunnel to Arch Street Friends Meeting House, connecting two stops on the Underground Railroad. Allen and wife Sarah also cared for escapees at their nearby home on

Richard Allen, founder of Mother Bethel A.M.E., still welcomes the faithful to church. Courtesy of P. Meyer for Visit Philadelphia

Spruce Street. The Allens are entombed in the modern church, which still hosts weekly services.

Walk one block to 6th Street. Turn right onto South Street.

Artist Willis Nomo Humphrey honors W.E.B. DuBois and the city's first African American firefighters. Courtesy of the South Street Headhouse District via Visit Philadelphia

9 Mapping Courage: Honoring the Legacy of W.E.B. Du Bois and Engine 11

601 South St.

◆ This mural honors Engine #11, the city's first all-black firehouse. The Philadelphia Fire Department was segregated when it was established in the 1870s. Engine #11 had 20 black firefighters, who were known as "leather lungs" as they were sent to the most dangerous fires. This mural also features W.E.B. DuBois, the activist and scholar who began a sociological study and count of black residents living in the city's seventh ward in 1899. DuBois was the first African American to receive a doctorate at Harvard University and was a founder of the National Association for the Advancement of Colored People (NAACP). To gather data for his census he knocked on at least 800 doors, speaking to thousands of residents, before publishing his results as a book, *The Philadelphia Negro.*

Continue west on South Street.

10 Octavius Catto Home

812 South Street

◆ Catto lived in the home at 812 South Street. He was assassinated on Election Day 1871, the first election after the 15th Amendment granted voting rights to all male citizens. Catto also led efforts to integrate the city's trolley cars, which had banned black passengers, kick-starting the movement by sitting on a horse-drawn trolley and refusing to leave. The driver and horses left, but Catto stayed all night, drawing others to his cause. Two years later, the city allowed blacks to use its public transportation system.

This statue of Octavius Catto voting on Election Day stands outside City Hall. Courtesy of E. Frizzelle for Visit Philadelphia

Catto's headstone reads, "The Forgotten Hero." In 2017, the city honored him with *A Quest for Parity*, a statue that shows Catto on his way to a ballot box.

Continue west on South Street. Turn left at South 9th Street, then turn right on Bainbridge Street.

The Institute for Colored Youth was the nation's first school exclusively for African Americans. Courtesy of Don Morfe for hmdb.org

11 Institute for Colored Youth

915 Bainbridge St.

❖ This was the country's first educational facility exclusively for African Americans. (Octavius Catto, a graduate, taught here.) Founded in 1840 with a $10,000 bequest by a Quaker philanthropist, the school was originally for orphan boys. When it moved to this location in 1866, it was co-ed and had expanded its educational offerings. Fanny Jackson Coppin, who taught Greek, Latin, and math, was an instructor who became the school's principal and later the first African American school superintendent in the country. In 1902, administrators moved the school to a 275-acre plot formerly owned by George Cheyney outside the city. The school eventually changed its name to Cheyney University.

Continue west on Bainbridge Street. Turn right on South Delhi Street.

12 William Still House and Underground Railroad Way Station

625 Delhi St.

❖ William Still, often called "the father of the Underground Railroad," and his wife, Letitia, owned the property, which is today a private home. "Within the house's narrow confines, they hid hundreds of escapees and gave well-known figures like Harriet Tubman shelter," WHYY.org noted in 2018. Still was a businessman and chairman of the Vigilance Committee of the Pennsylvania Anti-Slavery Society. In 1849, he received a large package that, when opened, revealed Henry "Box" Brown, an enslaved man from Virginia who had mailed himself to Philadelphia. Still kept a journal of the people he assisted between 1852 and 1857, titling each page "Arrived" then adding the person's name and a few biographical details. In 1872, he self-published their stories in *The Underground Railroad Records.*

William Still, the "father of the Underground Railroad," lived in this house.

Your walk ends here.

Did You Know?

Marian Anderson was banned from performing in Washington DC's Constitution Hall, but the Philadelphia native made history when she sang with the New York Philharmonic at the Lincoln Memorial in 1939. An estimated crowd of 75,000 gathered live and millions more listened via radio.

Native Philadelphian Paul Robeson was a civil rights activist, a stage and screen actor, a singer, a football player, a lawyer, and a gifted speaker. The son of a runaway slave, Robeson grew up in West Philadelphia, where his former home is a museum.

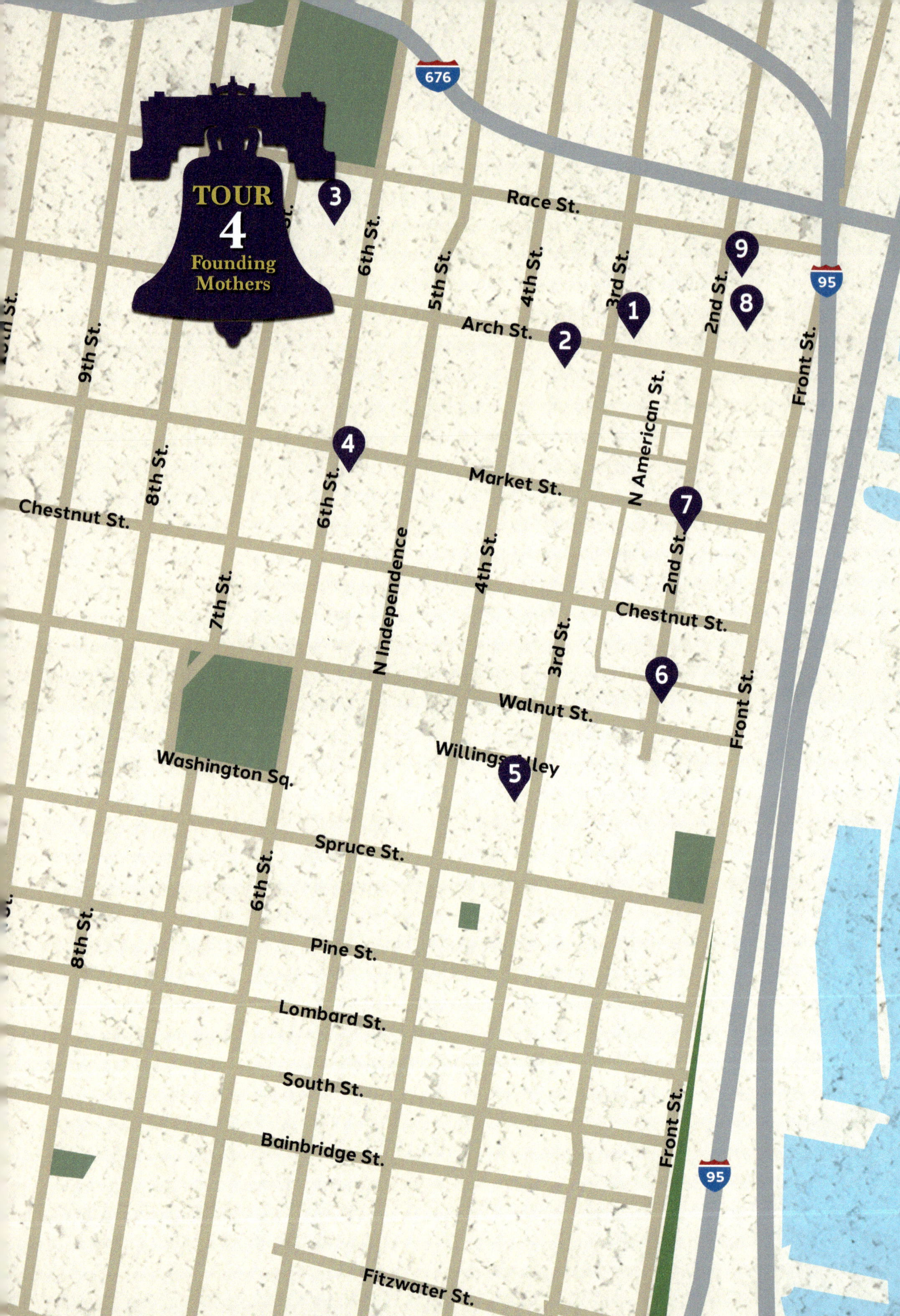

TOUR
4
Founding Mothers
676
95
Race St.
Arch St.
Market St.
Chestnut St.
Walnut St.
Willings
Washington Sq.
Spruce St.
Pine St.
Lombard St.
South St.
Bainbridge St.
Fitzwater St.
9th St.
8th St.
7th St.
6th St.
5th St.
N Independence
4th St.
3rd St.
N American St.
2nd St.
Front St.
1
2
3
4
5
6
7
8
9

TOUR 4
FOUNDING MOTHERS

Colonial women rarely made headlines. They had few rights, were banned from voting or inheriting property, and were meant to serve their husbands and children. The women in this walk were different. Most lived during colonial times, but one is a more modern hero. Or "she-ro."

1 Betsy Ross House
239 Arch St.

First flag maker Betsy Ross lived and worked here. Courtesy of Historic Philadelphia, Inc.

◆ First flag maker Betsy Ross personified patriotism and was nicknamed "the Little Rebel." She lost her first and second husbands during the war but never closed her busy upholstery shop, which packed ammunition and made musket balls along with tents and clothes for American soldiers.

 Walk one block west on Arch Street.

2 Arch Street Quaker Meeting House
320 Arch St.

◆ Abolitionists Sarah and Angelina Grimke worshipped here. They grew up in South Carolina where their father owned hundreds of enslaved people. In 1836, Angelina urged women to join the abolitionists: "I know you do not make the laws, but I also know that you are the wives and mothers, the sisters and daughters of those who do; and if

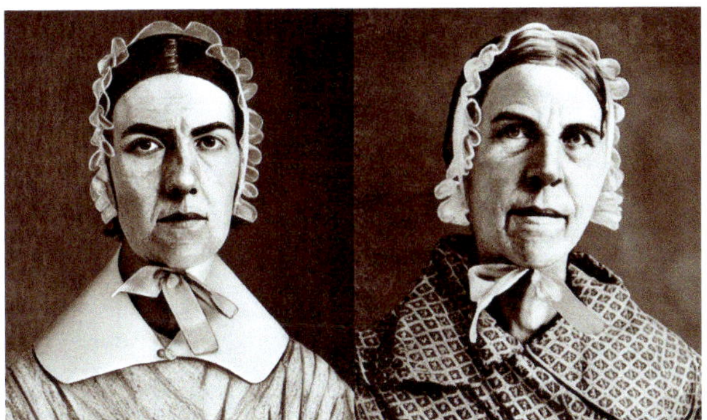
The Grimke sisters worshipped at Arch Street Quaker Meeting House.

you really suppose you can do nothing to overthrow slavery, you are greatly mistaken."

 Continue for three blocks on Arch Street.

3 Woman's Medical College of Pennsylvania
627 Arch St.

Woman's Medical College was the first degree-granting medical school for women in the country.

◆ Opened in 1850, the Woman's Medical College of Pennsylvania was the world's first all-female, degree-granting medical school. In 1870, female medical students who'd paid to attend a Pennsylvania Hospital lecture were heckled and spit on by male students. The incident positively shifted public opinion of female doctors. One female student said, "If these poor fellows had sought to do us a life-long favor, they could not have done it more effectively."

 Turn left on South 6th Street. Walk one block to Market Street.

GRANITE FREEMAN

Washington's Runaway Slave.

There is now living, in the borders of the town of Greenland N. H., *a runaway slave of* Gen. Washington, *at present supported by the County of Rockingham.* Her name, at the time of her elopement was Ona Maria Judge. She is not able to give the year of her escape but says that she came from Philadelphia, just after the close of Washington's second term of the Presidency, which must fix it somewhere in the first part of the year 1797. Being a waiting maid of Mrs. Washington, she was not exposed to any peculiar hardships. If asked why she did not remain in his service, she gives two reasons, first, that she wanted to be *free*, secondly, that she understood that after the decease of her master and mistress, she was to become the property of a grand-daughter of theirs, by the name of Custis, and that she was determined never to be her slave.

George Washington never stopped trying to recapture Oney Judge, the enslaved woman who served as Martha Washington's maid.

4 President's House
6th and Market Sts.

◆ Second First Lady Abigail Adams joined husband John here after he won the 1800 election. John often asked Abigail for advice, much to the displeasure of detractors, who called her "Mrs. President." When John attended the first Continental Congress, Abigail advised he "remember the ladies. . . . Do not put such unlimited powers in the hands of the husbands. Remember all men would be tyrants if they could." John's political rival, Thomas Jefferson, also sought Abigail's counsel.

Briefly close your eyes. Reopen them at the same site.

◆ **President's House, 6th and Market Sts.** Part of this museum is dedicated to the eight enslaved people the Washingtons held, including Oney Judge, who at age 12 became Martha Washington's "body servant." In 1796, Oney left the house while the Washingtons dined and fled to New England via ship. The Washingtons were outraged, feeling they'd treated Oney like family, and offered a reward for her capture. She died free in New Hampshire aged 75.

Turn left on Market Street. At South 3rd Street, turn right. Cross Walnut Street.

5 Powel House
244 S 3rd St.

◆ Samuel Powel was a politician, but his wife Elizabeth was the real power broker. A trusted advisor to George Washington, she urged him to reconsider when he balked at running for a second term, writing, "For Gods sake do not yield that Empire to a Love of Ease, Retirement, rural Pursuits, or a false Diffidence of Abilities which those that best know you so justly appreciate; nay your very Figure is calculated to inspire Respect and Confidence in the People . . ."

Elizabeth Powel was a close confidant of George Washington's. Painting by Matthew Pratt circa 1793

Return to Walnut Street. Turn left at South 2nd Street.

6 Welcome Park
127 S 2nd St.

◆ Hannah Callowhill Penn, wife of Pennsylvania founder William, was the state's first—and still only—female governor. She managed affairs for about 14 years, after her husband was incapacitated by strokes and after his death. While the Penns briefly lived in a house here, Hannah spent most of her life in England, governing via proxy. President Ronald Reagan made Penn an Honorary Citizen of the United States in 1984, noting that she'd "devoted her life to the pursuit of peace and justice."

Hannah Callowhill Penn in the house that stood here.

Continue north on South 2nd Street.

7 John Dunlap Print Shop
2nd and Market

◆ Esther de Berdt Reed hired this shop in 1780 to print "The Sentiments of an American Woman," calling for women to donate "vain ornaments" to support the war effort. Reed also founded the

Ladies Association of Philadelphia, intending to collect money for soldiers. George Washington, fearing troops would buy booze, asked instead for shirts. The women sewed more than 2,000, each embroidered with the maker's name. Thanking them, Washington wrote, "This fresh mark of the patriotism of the Ladies entitles them to the highest applause of their Country. It is impossible for the Army, not to feel a superior gratitude, on such an instance of goodness."

THE SENTIMENTS of an AMERICAN WOMAN.

ON the commencement of actual war, the Women of America manifested a firm resolution to contribute as much as could depend on them, to the deliverance of their country. …

… themselves into the flames rather than submit to the disgrace of humiliation before a proud enemy.

Esther de Berdt Reed had "The Sentiments of an American Woman" published here.

Cross Market Street. Continue north, crossing Arch Street.

Elfreth's Alley still exists today thanks to activist Dolley Ottey. Courtesy of C. Ridgeway for Visit Philadelphia

8 Elfreth's Alley

◆ Elfreth's Alley is the nation's oldest continuously inhabited residential street. The exteriors of the 32 houses lining a former cart path built between 1703 and 1836 remain unchanged thanks to Dolly Ottey, who launched the Elfreth's Alley Association in 1934. By that time, many of the houses were dilapidated, and some owners wanted to tear them down to erect larger dwellings. Ottey, a resident and business owner, successfully rallied her neighbors and saved the structures.

Continue north on North 2nd Street.

9 Elizabeth Drinker

147 N 2nd St.

Loyalist Elizabeth Drinker's diary provides insight into colonial life.

◆ Elizabeth Drinker's journals from 1758 to 1807 provide insight into the lives of ordinary Philadelphians during extraordinary times. Drinker and husband, Henry, were Quakers who stayed neutral during the Revolutionary War. In 1777, Henry Drinker and other prominent pacifists were arrested and charged with aiding the enemy by not fighting in the war. A few months later, Elizabeth Drinker and other women visited George Washington at Valley Forge to ask for their husbands' releases. Washington declined to do so, but he did serve an "elegant dinner."

Did You Know?

Many women, including Martha Washington, went to war with their husbands. These so-called "camp followers" performed domestic duties including cooking and washing.

Some women dressed as men to fight. One, Deborah Sampson of Massachusetts, served under her dead brother's name.

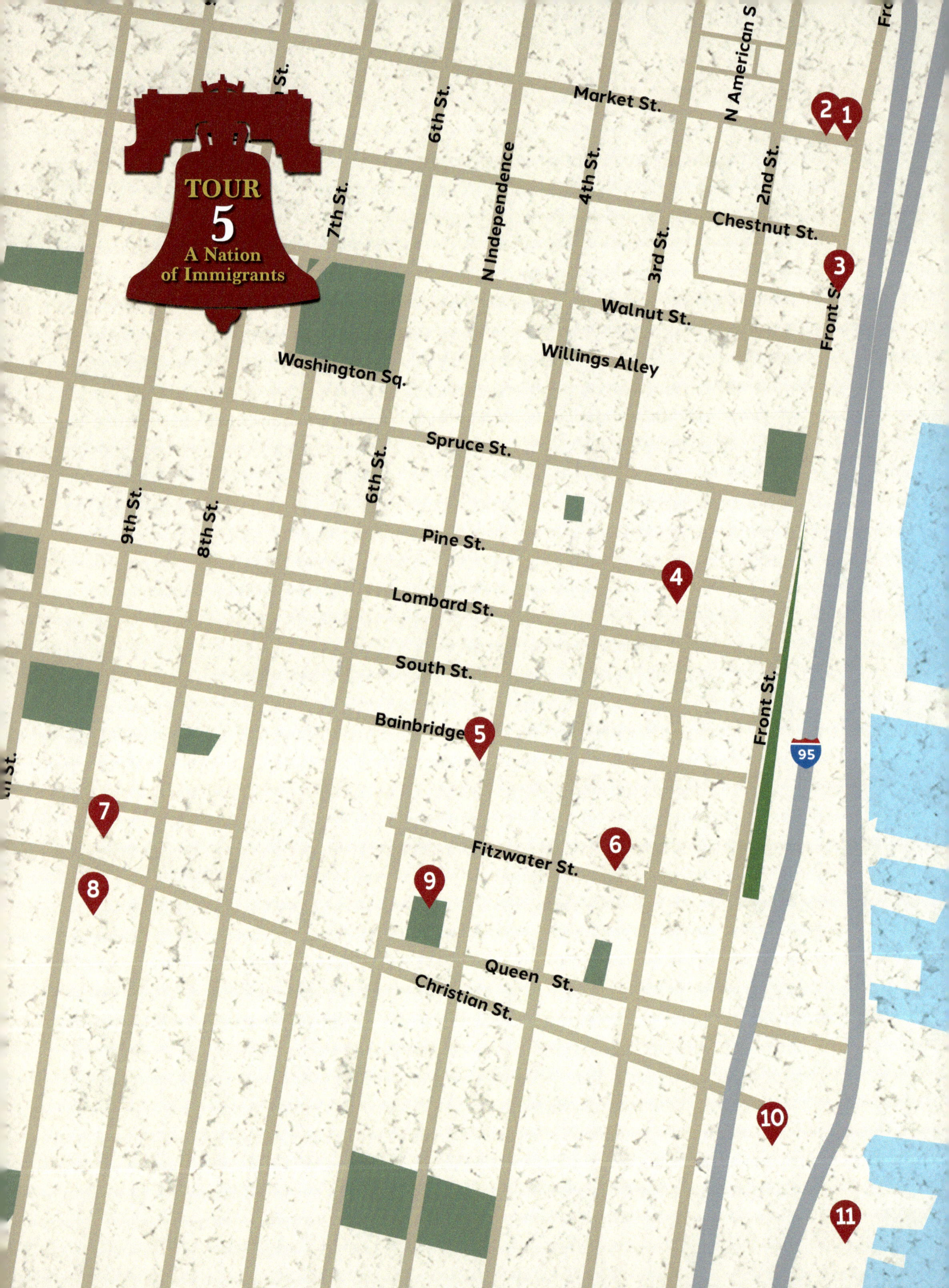
TOUR
5
A Nation of Immigrants
Market St.
N American S
2
1
6th St.
N Independence
4th St.
2nd St.
7th St.
Chestnut St.
3rd St.
3
Front St.
Walnut St.
Willings Alley
Washington Sq.
Spruce St.
6th St.
9th St.
8th St.
Pine St.
4
Lombard St.
South St.
Front St.
Bainbridge
5
95
7
6
Fitzwater St.
8
9
Queen St.
Christian St.
10
11

TOUR 5
A NATION OF IMMIGRANTS

Many of Philadelphia's original neighborhoods coalesced around immigrant communities. Between 1873 and 1915, more than one million immigrants, most European, arrived via the Washington Avenue Immigration Station. This walk includes locales related to those immigrants as well as enslaved Africans brought here against their will.

1 *Tamanend*
Front and Market Sts. (northside)

◆ Lenni-Lenape Chief Tamanend extends a hand in welcome to William Penn in 1682. An eagle on his shoulder carries a belt representing the agreement between the two that promised peace "as long as the waters run in the rivers and creeks and as long as the stars and moon endure." Tamanend translates to "Affable One," and some colonists called him "St. Tamanend."

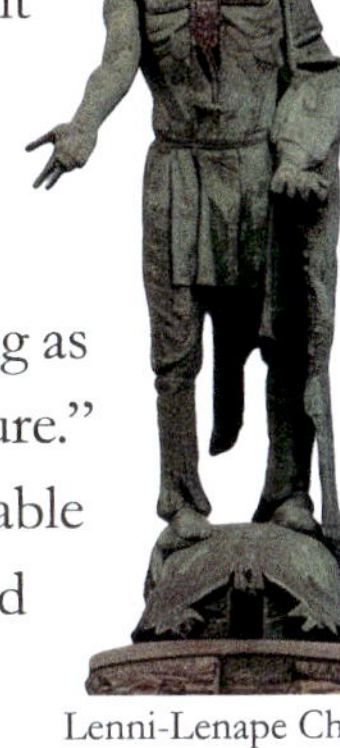
Lenni-Lenape Chief Tamanend. Courtesy of J.J. Prats for hmdb.org

Cross Market Street heading south.

2 London Coffee House
Front and Market Sts. (southside)

◆ Enslaved people were sold here during colonial times. *Common Sense* author Thomas Paine witnessed these sales in the 1770s and wrote an article calling for abolition, inspiring the first antislavery society. During the Revolutionary War, the coffeehouse was popular with British loyalists.

African Americans were sold as slaves at London Coffee House. Courtesy of Free Library of Philadelphia

Walk south on Front Street. Stop at Foglietta Plaza.

3 Commemoration of Scottish Immigration to America
I-95 Park, 109 Spruce St.

Monument to Scottish immigrants. Courtesy of William Fischer Jr. for hmdb.org

◆ This memorial, installed in 2011, recognizes the contributions of Scottish immigrants. A family, led by its Celtic Highland kilt-clad patriarch, arrives by boat. One figure wears colonial American garb, implying he arrived earlier to ease his family's transition. Scottish immigrants in Philadelphia were supported by the St. Andrew's Society, an organization named for Scotland's patron saint.

◆ In the same park stands the *Irish memorial, or An Corta Mor (The Great Hunger)*, commissioned to mark the famine's 150th anniversary. Millions of Irish died from starvation between 1845 and 1850, prompting thousands to immigrate. Peter Quinn's engraved poem begins, "The hunger ended/but it never went away/it was there in silent memories/from one generation/to the next . . ."

An Corta Mor remembers Ireland's Great Hunger. Courtesy of irishmemorial.org

Turn right on Spruce Street. Walk one block, then turn left on South 2nd Street.

4 Headhouse Square and the New Market, or the Shambles

S 2nd and Lombard Sts.

◆ Established in 1745, the market was built in the traditional British style, with 16 "shambles," or stalls, from which vendors sold foodstuffs, clothing, and other goods. This is the oldest surviving market of its kind in the US, and it is still in use. In the 1950s, the Headhouse was marked for destruction for a road project but saved by citizens' protests.

Continue south. At Lombard Street, turn right. At South 4th Street, turn left.

5 Famous 4th Street Delicatessen

700 S 4th St.

◆ When the deli opened in the 1920s, it was at the northern end of a thriving community of Jewish immigrants from eastern Europe and Russia who called it "Der Ferder," which means "Fourth" in Yiddish. The blocks south of the deli were heavy with pushcarts selling fabric and sewing supplies. Interspersed among the textile businesses were kosher butcher shops and other specialty stores. Talmud Torah, a school for boys, and a Yiddish theater were nearby.

Courtesy of C. Smyth for Visit Philadelphia

Continue south on South 4th Street. Turn left at Fitzwater Street.

6 St. Stanislaus Church

240 Fitzwater St.

◆ Polish immigrants disembarking at Washington Avenue Immigration Station often had the name "St. Stanislaus" written on pieces of paper pinned to their shirts so immigration workers knew to send them to St. Stanislaus Church. Opened in 1891 and named for Poland's patron saint, the church was built by its future congregants, many of whom "had little money, faced a frustrating language barrier, and worked ten to twelve hours a day for deplorable wages," according to the Philadelphia-based non-profit Polish American Center.

Walk back to South 4th Street and continue walking west. At South 9th Street, turn left.

7 Palumbo's/Italian Market

801 S 9th St.

◆ Just as Polish immigrants sought St. Stanislaus, many Italian immigrants arrived knowing only "Palumbo." In 1886, Antonio Palumbo opened a boardinghouse for newly arrived Italian immigrants. These settlers opened their own businesses, creating the "Italian Market," which runs about a mile along South 9th Street. Palumbo's grandson, Frank, converted the boardinghouse into a restaurant/nightclub that drew stars including Frank Sinatra as both diners and performers.

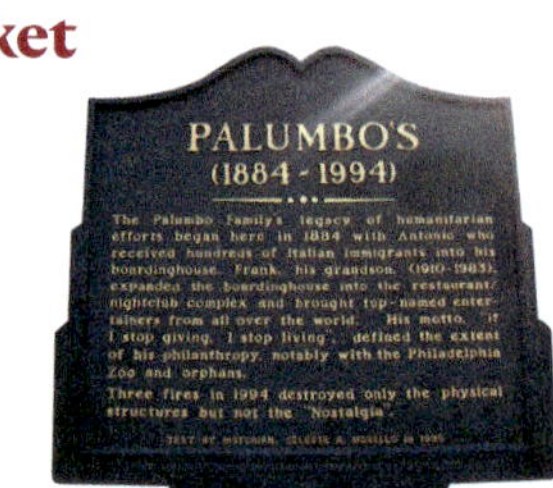

Sign marks former location of Palumbo's boardinghouse. Courtesy of AMP (Commons:Wiki Take Philadelphia project)

Walk south on South 9th Street. Stop at Christian Street.

8 The South 9th Street Italian Market

◆ South 9th Street between Fitzwater and Wharton Streets is one of the oldest and largest continuously operating outdoor markets in the US. In the first *Rocky* movie, the aspiring boxer is seen

Boarders at Palumbo's boarding house opened shops on South 9th Street, creating the South 9th Street Italian Market. Courtesy of Kelly for Visit Philadelphia

jogging on South 9th Street. One vendor throws him an orange, which he neatly catches. While the market still has a trademark grittiness, much has changed in the last century: Many of the shops are owned by new citizens from Mexico and southeast Asia.

Turn left on Christian Street. At South 5th Street, turn left again then make a right on Queen Street.

9 Weccacoe Playground

415 Queen St.

Land Buoy statue by Jody Pinto. Courtesy of M. Fischetti for Visit Philadelphia

◆ A 2013 upgrade uncovered the city's first private African American cemetery. Bethel Burial Ground was associated with nearby Mount Bethel A.M.E. church. Church records show that about 4,000 people were interred here between 1810 and 1864. Because of the limited space, coffins were stacked atop coffins. The first headstone recovered belonged to Amelia Brown, 26, who died in 1819. It read, "Whosoever live and believeth in me, though we be dead, so shall we live." By the 1980s, the cemetery was forgotten and used as a junkyard. The playground was installed a year later.

Continue east on South 4th Street. At Columbus Boulevard, turn right.

10 Gloria Dei (Old Swedes') Episcopal Church

916 S Swanson St.

◆ Swedish immigrants were the first Europeans to colonize the Delaware Valley. The church's first reverend helped build this church in 1700. The oldest tombstone in the cemetery, for Peter and Andreas Sandel, dates to 1708. The Swedish colonists were friendly with the native Lenni-Lenape, with one settler writing, "We live also in peace, friendship and amity with one another, and the indians have not molested us for many years."

Gloria Dei church. Courtesy of Visit Philadelphia

Continue west, then cross Columbus Boulevard at Washington Avenue. Follow the path to the Delaware River.

11 Washington Avenue Immigration Station

Washington Green, Washington Ave., and Columbus Blvd.

◆ Between 1873 and 1915, about a million European immigrants passed through the station, which was built by the Pennsylvania Railroad and promoted in European publications. Before ships docked, they stopped at a quarantine hospital a few miles south. An estimated 300 English-speaking or 150 non-English-speaking passengers were processed each hour.

Did You Know?

Between 1900 and 1920, when many blacks living in the south moved north as part of the Great Migration, Philadelphia's black population more than doubled, increasing from 63,000 to 134,000.

Philadelphia continues to be a proud city of immigrants. The mayor's office says 180 different languages are spoken here.

Tour
6
Penn's
"Holy
Experiment"
676
Race St.
Arch St.
Market St.
Chestnut St.
Chestnut St.
Walnut St.
Willings Alley
Washington Sq.
Spruce St.
Pine St.
Lombard St.
South St.
Bainbridge St.
Fitzwater St.
Queen St.
Christian St.
10th St.
9th St.
8th St.
8th St.
7th St.
7th St.
6th St.
6th St.
6th St.
5th St.
N Independence
4th St.
4th St.
3rd St.
3rd St.
2nd St.
2nd St.
N American St.
Front St.
Front St.
Front St.
95
95
1
2
3
4
5
6
7
8
9
10
11

TOUR 6
PENN'S "HOLY EXPERIMENT"

William Penn considered Philadelphia his "Holy Experiment," a place where people with different religious beliefs could worship as they wished without fear of reprisals. Before arriving in the New World in 1682, Penn had been imprisoned for sharing the teachings of the Society of Friends in public and in publication. Society of Friends believers are better known as Quakers, but the name was meant to be an insult, an eye-rolling reference to church members who sometimes shook with fervor during Friends' meetings. This walk will take you to a few of the city's earliest places of worship.

Gloria Dei/Old Swede's church has a Swedish-made baptismal font.
Courtesy of B. Krist for Visit Philadelphia

1 Gloria Dei/Old Swede's
916 S Swanson St.

◆ Gloria Dei/Old Swede's is the oldest church in Pennsylvania. The native Lenni-Lenape called this area "Weccaco," which means "peaceful place." When Swedish colonists settled here in the 1640s, they dubbed the area "New Sweden." Construction on this church was completed in 1704. It originally served a Lutheran congregation, joining the Episcopal church in the 1840s. This building contains a baptismal font and wood carvings imported from Sweden. The church's neighboring cemetery has been active since the early 1700s. While the church is only 1.5 miles from Independence Hall, it was originally outside the city's borders. Christian Street is named in honor of Sweden's Queen Christina, and the surrounding neighborhood is called Queen Village.

Walk west on Christian Street. At South 2nd Street, turn right. Continue to Market Street.

Christ Church has been called "the nation's church."
Courtesy of M. Kennedy for Visit Philadelphia

2 Christ Church
20 N American St.

◆ Christ Church is considered "the birthplace of the American Episcopal Church." It was founded in 1695, the first Church of England parish in Pennsylvania. Many Founding Mothers and Fathers attended its services, including Deborah and Benjamin Franklin, and are interred at its nearby cemetery. Christ Church has also been called "the nation's church" and "the church of the American

Revolution." Its "Chime of Eight Bells" sounded on July 8, 1776, to summon people to the first public reading of the Declaration of Independence. Congregants smuggled the bells out of town on the first night of the British occupation of Philadelphia in September 1777 so the Redcoats couldn't use the metal for ammunition.

Turn left on Market Street. At 4th Street, turn right.

3 St. George's United Methodist Church

235 N 4th St.

◆ St. George's United Methodist Church opened in 1769, making it the country's oldest Methodist church in continuous use. Its faithful are Christians who try to follow the teachings of John Wesley, a priest, and Charles Wesley, a student, who in the 1720s began hosting daily Bible studies and services at Oxford University. The church has three main tenets: Do no harm. Do good. Love God. Like "Quakers," the term "Methodists" was meant to be an insult, implying practitioners were too rigid in their worship. As another Methodist church notes, "John Wesley was wholly unpopular at every phase of his life. . . . At every turn people who thought they were smarter, more spiritual, more doctrinally sound tried to invalidate his efforts and what he represented."

St. George's Methodist Church is the country's oldest continuously operational Methodist church. Courtesy of the Historic St. George's Methodist Church for Visit Philadelphia

The Arch Street Meeting House is still an active place of worship. Courtesy of M. Fischetti for Visit Philadelphia

Turn around and walk south back to Market Street. Turn right on Market Street. At South 5th Street, turn left.

4 Free Quaker Meeting House/Arch Street Friends Meeting House

500 Arch St.

◆ Pacifism is a tenet of the Quaker faith. Most Philadelphia Quakers believed that the conflicts between the British crown and its 13 American colonies could be resolved without violence. Most, but not all. About 200 Friends supported the war and wanted to fight, and for that they were "read out of meeting," meaning expelled from their places of worship. The castoffs renamed themselves the "Free Quakers" and began worshipping here in 1783, the final year of the Revolutionary War. The University of Pennsylvania's mascot is a Quaker, and its athletes have the oxymoronic nickname "fighting Quakers."

Continue walking south.

5 Mikveh Israel

44 N 4th St.

◆ Mikveh Israel has been called "the synagogue of the American Revolution." (While its address is on South 4th Street, enter the synagogue property near the Uriah P. Levy statue.) Before the congregation

Mikveh Israel

was established in 1740, Jewish faithful worshipped at home. It is the oldest synagogue in continuous use in the nation. It settled in this location in 1976. (This is the congregation's fifth location. Its cemetery is blocks away at South 8th and Spruce Streets.) Among the synagogue's early congregants: Uriah P. Levy, the Navy's first Jewish commodore, and Haym Solomon, a financier of the Revolutionary War who died penniless. To pay off its own building loans, the synagogue asked "worthy Citizens of every religious Denomination" for contributions. Benjamin Franklin and George Washington were among those who donated.

Continue walking south to Walnut Street. At Walnut Street, turn left. Walk one more block and turn right onto Willings Alley.

6 Old St. Joe's
321 Willings Alley

When it opened in 1733, Old St. Joe's was the only place in the English-speaking world where Roman Catholics could publicly and legally attend Mass. Courtesy of Old St. Joseph's

◆ When Old St. Joe's Church was founded in 1733, it was the only place in the English-speaking world where Roman Catholics could publicly and legally attend Mass. While William Penn aimed to build a city where Christian religions could coexist peacefully, there was always an uneasiness directed at those deemed "different," as the Quakers were in England. Benjamin Franklin reportedly advised the church's first pastor to tone down the traditional Catholic glitz seen in Europe. This church was spared during anti-Catholic riots in the 1840s that killed one man and destroyed a dozen buildings. The church has links to two saints: St. Katharine Drexel, who taught Sunday school, and St. John Neumann, who visited while Bishop of Philadelphia.

Continue walking west on Willings Alley. At South 4th Street, turn left.

7 Old St. Mary's
248 S 4th St.

Commodore Barry worshipped at Old St. Mary's Church.

◆ Old St. Mary's was built in 1763 to host Sunday overflow services for congregants of Old St. Joseph's Church. The first Continental Congress gathered here at least four times, and the second Continental Congress came here for the first public religious celebration of the Declaration of Independence. Famous parishioners included Commodore John Barry, who is often called the "Father of the US Navy" because of his success in battle and who oversaw the construction of its first six frigates. As captain of the *Lexington* during the Revolutionary War, he was the first to capture an enemy ship. Barry is interred in the neighboring cemetery. Old St. Mary's was combined with Holy Trinity in 2009.

Continue walking south on South 4th Street. At Spruce Street, turn right. Stop at South 6th Street.

Holy Trinity Church was built by German Catholics.

8 Holy Trinity Church
S 6th and Spruce Sts.

◆ German-speaking Catholics built this church in 1789, making it the country's first ethnic parish. The church ran the country's first orphanage, taking in children who had lost parents during the yellow fever epidemic of 1793. Poetry fans have been known to search the church's neighboring cemetery for the graves of Evangeline and Gabriel, the ill-fated lovers in Henry Wadsworth Longfellow's epic poem "Evangeline." They don't exist, but many believe Longfellow, who visited the city twice, was referring to Holy Trinity when he described "the little Catholic churchyard in the heart of the city." Holy Trinity was combined with Old St. Mary's in 2009.

Turn left on South 6th Street, walking south. At Pine Street, turn left.

9 Old Pine Street Church
412 Pine St.

◆ The church is called "Church of the Patriots." One early leader, George Duffield, was an outspoken supporter of American independence. His anti-British feelings were so well-known that

Old Pine St. Church is called "the church of the Patriots" because of the fervor of its minister, George Duffield. Courtesy of Old Pine Street Church

King George III reportedly offered a reward of $50 to anyone who could capture Duffield, dead or alive. Duffield traveled with the Continental Army, serving as chaplain when Washington's troops hunkered down in Valley Forge in the winter of 1776. In the 2010s, the church removed a 100-year-old dead tree on its property but left its stump for sculptor Roger Wing to carve into a likeness of Duffield. He carries a Bible in one hand. The other has two fingers raised in the sign of peace.

Continue walking east on Pine Street.

10 St. Peter's Church
313 Pine St.

◆ The church was opened in 1761 to accommodate worshippers who felt crowded at nearby Christ Church. Both institutions were led by Reverend William White, the chaplain for the Second Continental Congress and the first bishop of the American Episcopal Church. Christ Church faithful, including John Adams, also attended services at St. Peter's. As with many churches of the time, the interior has box pews, many belonging to individual families and priced according to location.

St. Peter's Church was opened to handle Christ Church overflow.

The structure helped worshippers stay warm before the advent of central heating as box owners could bring warm coals to services. St. Peter's is one of the few modern churches that still has box pews; most have converted their interiors to rows of benches.

Continue east on Pine Street. At South 6th Street, turn left.

11 Mother Bethel African Methodist Episcopal Church

419 S 6th St.

◆ Mother Bethel African Methodist Episcopal Church is the world's first church of its kind. Founder Richard Allen was born into slavery but later bought his freedom for $2,000. He became a respected preacher and the Episcopal church's first African American ordained minister. Allen first led services at St. George's Methodist Church but was frustrated by the church's segregationist policies. About 40 of St. George's faithful, known as "Allenites," followed him to his new church. The church was a stop on the Underground Railroad, with ushistory.org noting that Allen and his wife "would hide, feed and clothe escaping slaves. . . . Some current members of the Mother Bethel AME church are descendants of those who were escaped slaves assisted by Mother Bethel."

Mother Bethel African Methodist Church is the nation's first AME church. Courtesy of P. Meyer for Visit Philadelphia

One of Pennsylvania's nicknames is "The Quaker State." It has the largest concentration of practicing Quakers in the US.

The Pew Research Center says about 68 percent of Philadelphians self-identify as Christians. The second-largest group, at 24 percent, is "Irreligion," people who are lacking or indifferent to religious beliefs.

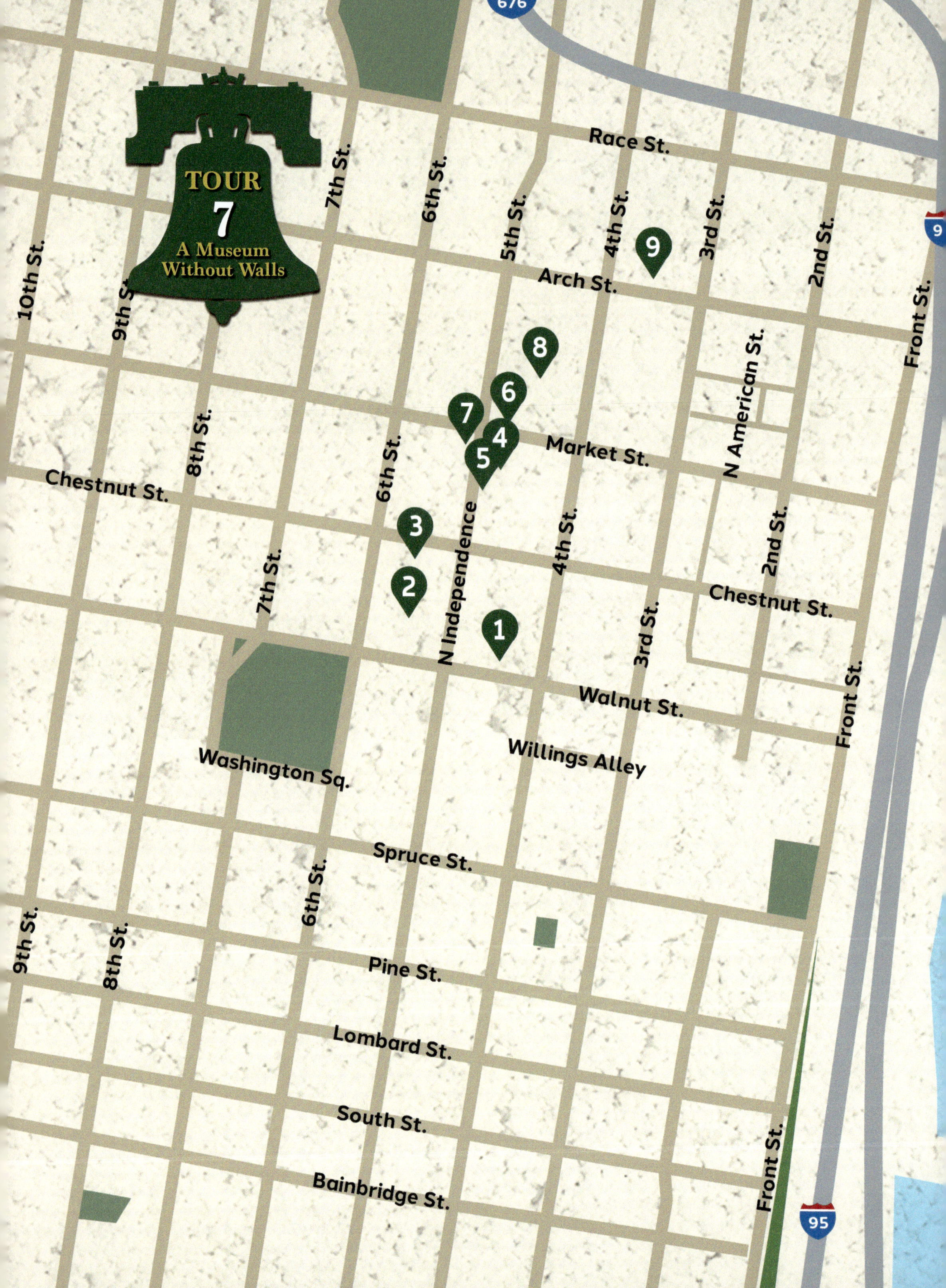

TOUR
7
A Museum Without Walls
676
Race St.
Arch St.
Market St.
Chestnut St.
Chestnut St.
Walnut St.
Willings Alley
Washington Sq.
Spruce St.
Pine St.
Lombard St.
South St.
Bainbridge St.
10th St.
9th St.
8th St.
7th St.
6th St.
5th St.
4th St.
3rd St.
2nd St.
Front St.
N American St.
N Independence
6th St.
7th St.
4th St.
3rd St.
2nd St.
Front St.
9th St.
8th St.
6th St.
Front St.
95
1
2
3
4
5
6
7
8
9

TOUR 7
A MUSEUM WITHOUT WALLS

Philadelphia has one of the largest public art collection in the world. Its revolutionary Mural Arts program has created more than 4,000 murals since launching in 1986. The nonprofit Association for Public Art, the nation's first public arts support organization, is dedicated to "integrating public art and urban design." Since 1959, the Philadelphia Redevelopment Authority has required new construction and major redevelopment projects to donate 1 percent of their budgets for public art.

1 *Robert Morris*
412 Walnut St.

◆ The statue honors one of the lesser-known Founding Fathers who was called "the Financier of the Revolution" and signed both the Declaration of Independence and the US Constitution. A close confidant of George Washington's, Morris was one of the nation's first millionaires, making his fortune in international trade. In 1776, Washington wrote to Morris asking if he could raise $10,000 for Washington's exhausted troops. Morris gave $10,000 of his own money. This boost provided much-needed provisions for soldiers as they crossed the Delaware River into New Jersey and defeated the British at the Battle of Trenton. After the war, Morris made bad investments and ended up in debtors' prison about two blocks from this statue. Washington often visited.

Robert Morris, the so-called financier of the Revolutionary War, later ended up broke and in prison. Courtesy of Carol M. Highsmith/Library of Congress

Walk north to South 5th Street. Follow the diagonal path heading northwest.

2 *Commodore John Barry*
111 S Independence Mall W

◆ The statue honors the "Father of the United States Navy." Barry's contributions to the Revolutionary War efforts "are unparalleled," notes ushistory.org. Among them: A ship helmed by Barry "was the first to capture a British war vessel on the high seas; he captured two British ships after being severely wounded in a ferocious sea battle; he quelled three mutinies; he fought on land at the Battles of Trenton and Princeton; he captured more than 20 ships, including an armed British schooner in the lower Delaware; and he fought the last naval battle of the American Revolution aboard the frigate Alliance in 1783." A native of Ireland, Barry is interred at Old St. Mary's Church.

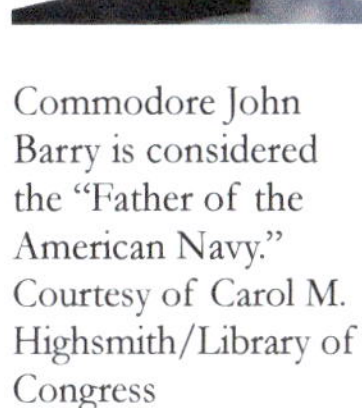

Commodore John Barry is considered the "Father of the American Navy." Courtesy of Carol M. Highsmith/Library of Congress

Return to South 5th Street via the straight path on the right. At Chestnut Street, turn left.

3 *George Washington* Independence Hall
Chestnut St. between S 5th and S 6th Sts.

◆ The statue is a bronze replica of the white marble original dedicated in 1869. In 1934, the *Philadelphia Inquirer* noted that the original work, now at City Hall, "has two fingers held on with adhesive tape, a

This statue of George Washington was originally cast in 1869. Courtesy of the National Park Service

wig that is filled with cobwebs and its sword handle is entirely missing." Sculptor Joseph Alexis Bailly was a French-born Philadelphia transplant. He was briefly an instructor at the Pennsylvania Academy of the Fine Arts. Other notable works by Bailly include a statue of John Witherspoon that in Fairmount Park. Witherspoon was the only active clergyman who signed the Declaration of Independence.

Return to South 5th Street. Turn left.

4 *Religious Liberty*, Weitzman National Museum of American Jewish History

101 S Independence Mall E (S 5th and Market Sts.)

◆ This is the country's largest monument to freedom of religion, erected in 1876 to celebrate the nation's centennial. Sculptor Moses Jacob Ezekiel trained in Rome and used ancient Roman symbols in his work. As theweitzman.org details, the woman is wearing both a toga and protective armor. She carries a laurel wreath, representing victory, and a bundle of birch rods, which symbolizes power. The eagle, symbolic of the US, is using its talons to choke a serpent, representing the British monarchy. Ezekiel was the first Jewish graduate of the Virginia Military Academy and fought for the Union during the Civil War.

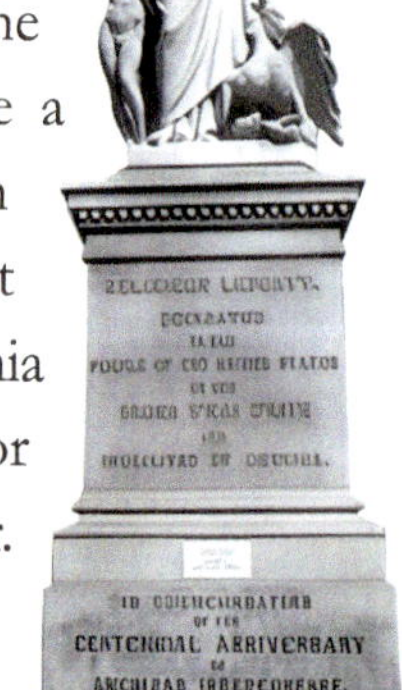

Religious Liberty, made for the nation's centennial celebration, is a reference to William Penn's "Holy Experiment." Courtesy of Wikimedia Commons

After the war, he took commissions for both Union and Confederate monuments.

Walk north a few more steps on South 5th Street.

5 *OY/YO*—Weitzman National Museum of American Jewish History

101 S Independence Mall (S 5th and Market Sts.)

◆ This is one of the city's newer pieces of outdoor art, installed in 2022. As billypenn.com notes, Deborah Kass's work "shouts a perfect Philly welcome to people lining up to see the Liberty Bell: 'Yo!' . . . Viewed from the other side, however, it has an equally appropriate message for our times: 'Oy!'" Kass says the sculpture speaks to "the American promise of equality and fairness and our responsibilities to make the country a better place for all." The aluminum statue, painted "Lamborghini yellow," is one of several copies of this work. Others can be found in Brooklyn and in Stanford, California.

Continue north, crossing Market Street.

6 *Gift of the Winds*

401–499 Market St.

◆ This is one of the works created to fulfill the city's public art requirement for developers. Sculptor Joseph C. Bailey, a former member of the Philadelphia Arts Commission, has pieces on display throughout Philadelphia. When this 17-foot, polished stainless steel and bronze work was installed 300 yards from the Liberty Bell in 1979, it was the first work by a black sculptor on Independence Mall. When Bailey died in 1994, a *Philadelphia Inquirer* articled described him as "a creator of monuments and almost one himself in the city's art world."

Continue north to North 5th Street.

7 *Commodore Uriah Phillips Levy*
S 5th and Market Sts.

◆ This statue remembers a man who identified himself thusly: "I am an American, a sailor, and a Jew." Levy, who celebrated his bar mitzvah here, was the US Navy's first Jewish commodore. During the Civil War, President Abraham Lincoln appointed Levy to the Navy's Court Martial Board, where he was instrumental in ending the practice of flogging wayward sailors. The board was also the first military organization in the world to abolish capital punishment, according to philart.net. Because of antisemitism, Levy was court-martialed six times, demoted to captain once, and twice dismissed from the Navy. He fought his dismissal and was allowed to rejoin the Navy in 1855.

Cross Market Street. At the entrance of Mikveh Israel synagogue, turn right onto the property.

8 *Jonathan Netanyahu Memorial*
N 5th St.

◆ The memorial honors "Yoni" Netanyahu, brother of Benjamin, who was killed in 1976 leading Israeli troops that rescued 103 hostages after a hijacking. In June, terrorists affiliated with Palestine and Germany took control of a Paris-bound Air France flight, diverting the plane first to Libya, then to Uganda. Their demands included a $5 million ransom. On July 3–4, Netanyahu led the team that freed the hostages. He died along with three hostages and seven hijackers. A Cheltenham High School classmate led efforts to install the memorial, telling the *Philadelphia Inquirer* at its 1986 unveiling that Netanyahu was "almost superhuman. He is a tragic hero. The event in which he died . . . should be memorialized." The white slabs symbolize his strength and purity.

Continue walking east through Mikveh Israel's grounds. At South 4th Street, turn left. At Arch Street, turn right.

9 *History of the Philadelphia Fire Department*
323 Arch St.

◆ The mural is just that, tracing the company's history from the volunteer squad cocreated by Benjamin Franklin in 1736 to the present day. Featured images include Isaac Jacobs, the first black firefighter, hired in 1886; fire response vehicles through history; and a frieze of St. Florian, the patron saint of firefighters. Also here is *Keys to Community*, a bronze sculpture of Franklin made with 1,000 keys provided by local schoolchildren. The sculptor wanted it to look as if Franklin was turning to greet a visitor.

It's fitting that a bust of Benjamin Franklin, *Keys to Community*, was made with more than 1,000 keys donated by schoolchildren. Courtesy of Bill Coughlin for hmdb.org

Did You Know?

In 2025, Philadelphia was honored with first place in *USA Today*'s 10Best Readers' Choice Award for Best City for Street Art. It won in the same category in 2023.

Philadelphia street artist Darryl McCray, better known as "Cornbread," is called "the godfather of graffiti" and "the king of walls."

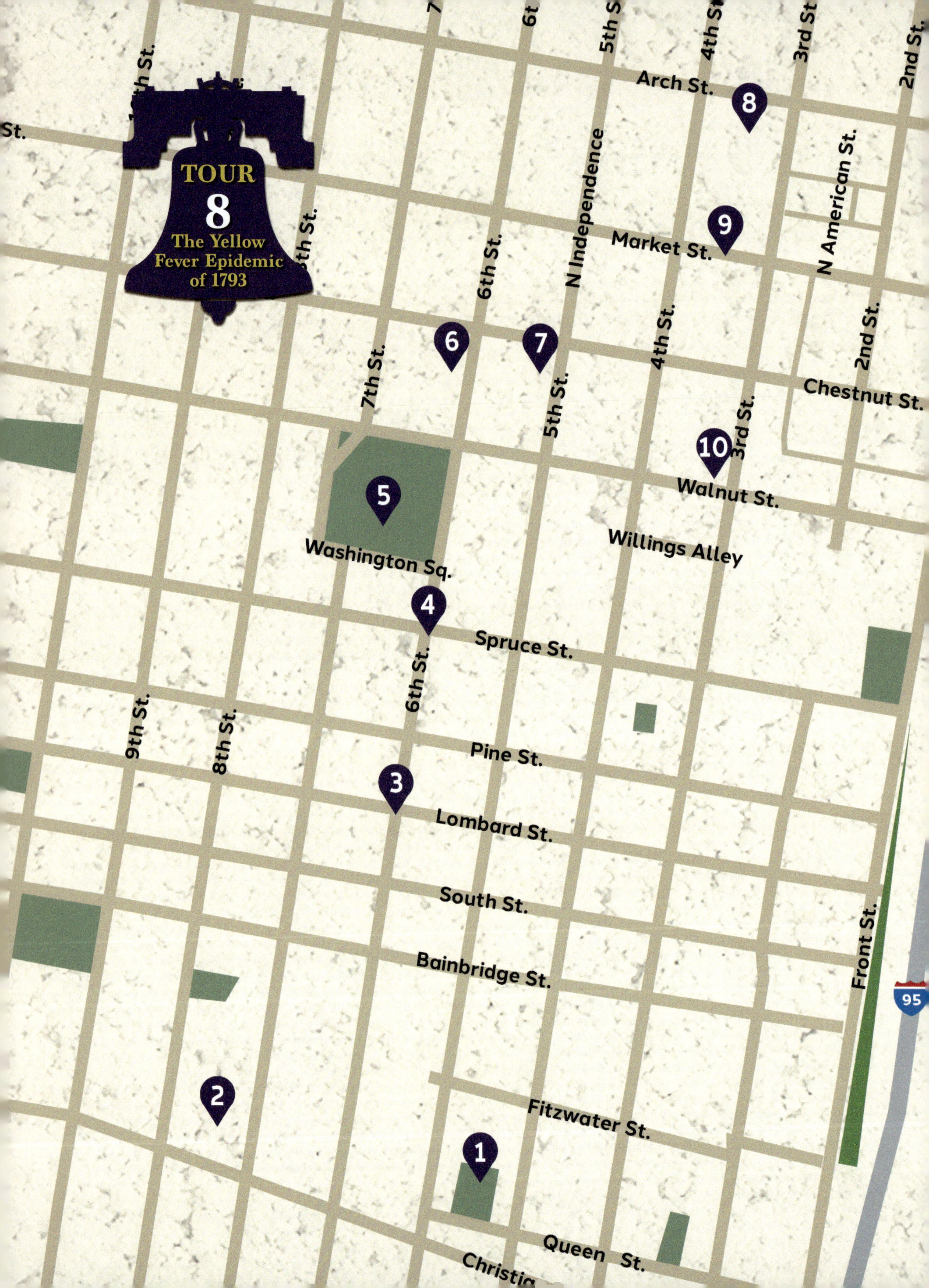
TOUR
8
The Yellow
Fever Epidemic
of 1793
Arch St.
Market St.
Chestnut St.
Walnut St.
Willings Alley
Washington Sq.
Spruce St.
Pine St.
Lombard St.
South St.
Bainbridge St.
Fitzwater St.
Queen St.
N Independence
N American St.
2nd St.
3rd St.
4th St.
5th St.
6th St.
7th St.
8th St.
9th St.
Front St.
95
1
2
3
4
5
6
7
8
9
10

TOUR 8
THE YELLOW FEVER EPIDEMIC OF 1793

The yellow fever epidemic of 1793 shaped the Philadelphia we know today. At the time, Philadelphia was the nation's capital, its largest city with about 50,000 residents, and one of its busiest ports. Between August and November of 1793, the disease killed 5,000 residents. Those who could afford to leave the city did so, and the mayor estimated the number who fled at about 17,000 people. Among them were George Washington and his cabinet, who traveled 10 miles northwest to what was then the suburb of Germantown but is now part of the city. Colonials weren't sure what caused the deadly disease, but some believed polluted drinking water or streets filled with animal waste were to blame.

In truth, yellow fever arrived in the US via the Delaware River port, when ships from Haiti brought in infected individuals fleeing the Haitian Revolution. Mosquitoes then spread the disease throughout the city.

Pennysylvania Hospital

1 Weccacoe Playground/Old Bethel Burial Ground
400 Catharine St.

◆ Prominent physician Benjamin Rush, a signer of the Declaration of Independence, believed that African Americans were immune to the fever, prompting him to ask the Free African Society to recruit caregivers from its membership. Sarah Bass Allen, second wife of AME church founder Richard Allen, quickly stepped forward. Formerly enslaved, Allen cared for white strangers throughout the pandemic. She survived the fever and was buried here in 1849 after her death at age 87. She was later reinterred at Mt. Bethel A.M.E. church, where her husband rests. The Allens were also conductors of the Underground Railroad. You'll learn more about them at your third stop.

Walk west on Catharine Street.

2 House of Industry
714 Catharine St.

◆ Ann Parish was 33 years old in 1793. She lost two of her brothers to the epidemic before her parents, too, became ill. Ann, a Quaker, prayed for their recovery, promising to devote herself to charity if they survived. When they lived, she cofounded first the Female Society for the Relief of the Distressed to care for victims of the epidemic, then the House of Industry to provide female survivors with work and childcare. Ann's goodness did not go unrecognized. Close friend Catharine Morris later wrote that Ann "was exemplary in fulfilling the Commands of her Savior, in visiting the Sick, feeding the Hungry, and clothing the Naked—and many were the Hours she passed in seeking out the Habilitation of the disconsolate

Portrait of Ann Parish. Courtesy of Free Library of Philadelphia

Widow, and wiping the artless tear of sorrow from the Eye of the innocent orphan."

Return to South 7th Street. Turn left. At Lombard Street, turn right.

3 Free African Society
S 6th and Lombard Sts.

◆ Society founders Richard Allen and Absalom Jones encouraged their members to step up during the epidemic, by caring for the sick, burying the dead, and building coffins. They hoped their efforts would raise the standing of African Americans in Philadelphia society. Instead, after the fever's end, some of their volunteers were accused of overcharging for their nursing services and stealing property from the afflicted. Allen and Jones sought to end the rumors by publishing 1794's *A Narrative of the Proceedings of the Black People, During the Late Awful Calamity in Philadelphia in the Year 1793 and a Refutation of Some Censures, Thrown upon them in some late Publications.* Dr. Rush's belief that African Americans had natural immunity to yellow fever proved false, as records show they died at the same rate as whites.

Walk north on South 6th Street.

Holy Trinity Roman Catholic Church. Courtesy of the Library of Congress

4 Holy Trinity Church
S 6th and Spruce Sts.

◆ The church founded the nation's first Catholic orphanage to care for children orphaned by yellow fever. It is also the final resting place of Stephen Girard, the wealthy merchant who managed Bush Hill, a yellow fever hospital in a mansion outside the city limits. Girard, who easily could have afforded to leave the city, instead threw himself into the work, transforming a dirty, chaotic clinic into a functioning hospital. Girard rejected Dr. Rush's harsh treatment methods. Instead, he "gave his charges wine and lemonade, staffed the hospital with French emigres, spent his own fortune to maintain it, emphasized cleanliness, and himself nursed the sick and buried the dead," according to *Philadelphia Magazine*.

Continue north on South 6th Street.

Washington Square. Courtesy of the National Park Service

5 Washington Square

◆ More than 1,300 yellow fever victims were buried in Washington Square, joining the Revolutionary War soldiers, indigent individuals, and enslaved Africans already interred there. At one point, the square's caretaker said that he personally had dug graves for more than 1,000 bodies here and near Bush Hill. A few years later, a wealthy developer purchased land along the square and built the city's first uniformly designed set of row houses. (The project's architect, Benjamin LaTrobe, would later design Fairmount Water Works, the first-of-its-kind municipal water supply facility that was as beautiful as it was practical, becoming a tourist attraction in later years.) Individuals who purchased these homes asked the city to transform the burial ground outside their front doors into a park. In 1825, the newly named Washington Square had more than 200 trees.

Continue north on South 6th Street. Cross Walnut Street.

6 Loganian Library
S 6th St. between Walnut and Chestnut Sts.

Loganian Library. Courtesy of the Library of Congress

◆ In 1792, this building became a temporary shelter for children whose parents were ill or had died. During its months of operation, it housed 192 children. Of those, 27 died from the fever.

Successful merchant James Logan, who one biographer called "the greatest bookman of colonial America," had this structure built to house his collection of more than 2,600 books, many in Latin or Greek. Logan, who also served as mayor of Philadelphia and chief justice of Pennsylvania, once said that "Books are my disease." His library reopened to the public after the pandemic.

Continue north to Chestnut Street. Turn right.

7 Old City Hall
S 5th and Chestnut Sts.

◆ While most people of means fled the city during the fever outbreak, Mayor Matthew Clarkson did not, recognizing that the city needed a leader who would rise to the occasion. Clarkson asked "benevolent citizens" to come to Old City Hall to join a group of citizens who would help him guide the city through the crisis. In the fashion of the time, the committee's name was as long as its mandate: Committee to Attend to and Alleviate the Suffering of the Afflicted with the Malignant Fever Prevalent

Philadelphia Old City Hall. Courtesy of the Library of Congress

in the City and its Vicinity. These volunteers were tasked with patient care, burying the dead, and caring for orphans. Some died from the fever.

Walk north on South 5th Street. At Arch Street, turn right.

8 Arch Street Meeting House
320 Arch St.

Arch Street Meeting House. Courtesy of the Library of Congress

◆ The burial ground at Arch Street Meeting House was nearly at its 20,000-person capacity when yellow fever struck. Still, victims were buried here, sometimes as the second or third body in a single grave. Early Quaker cemeteries like this one were unique in that they welcomed church members as

well as "Indians, Blacks and strangers," as the meetinghouse's website notes. Early Quakers didn't use headstones or grave markers, believing that doing so would "draw excessive attention to oneself and [be] seen as 'inconsistent with the plainness of our Principles and Practice.'" That practice changed in the late 1800s.

Continue east on Arch Street. At North 3rd Street, turn right. At Market Street, turn left, walking west.

9 Mathew Carey House
324 Market St.

◆ Printer and prominent citizen Mathew Carey had his home and business here. He promoted the idea that African American caregivers had actually taken advantage of dying yellow fever patients. His pamphlet, *A Short Account of the Malignant Fever Lately Prevalent in Philadelphia*, made the following accusation: "The great demand for nurses afforded an opportunity for imposition, which was eagerly seized by some of the vilest of the blacks. They extorted two, three, four, and even five dollars a night for attendance, which would have been well paid by a single dollar." Some were confused by Carey's stance, as he was an ardent abolitionist and had lost a child to yellow fever.

Double back on Market Street to South 3rd Street. Turn right, walking south.

10 Benjamin Rush House
198 S 3rd St.

◆ Declaration of Independence signer Dr. Rush was one of the most highly regarded medical practitioners of his day, but he got it all wrong when it came to yellow fever. He believed the mosquito-born disease was spread person-to-person, and the best treatments included using mercury to induce vomiting and substantial bloodletting. His ideas put him at odds with other leading physicians, who (correctly) believed that the best treatment included rest, fluids, and fresh air. Dr. Rush held tightly to his beliefs, even after losing three assistants to the disease and becoming gravely ill himself. He recovered but was so angered by the opposition to his methods that he resigned from the College of Physicians, which he'd cofounded in 1787.

Did You Know?

Major port cities including New York and Baltimore established quarantines against people and goods of Philadelphia.

Still, yellow fever could not be contained. It hit Baltimore in 1794, New York in 1795, and Boston in 1798, prompting one doctor to call it the most pressing national problem of the early nation.

Sources

Print

Aden, Roger. *Upon the Ruins of Liberty*. Philadelphia: Temple University Press, 2014.

Anderson, Laurie Halse. *Fever* 1793. New York: Simon and Schuster, 2000

Colimore, Edward. *The Philadelphia Inquirer's Walking Tours*. Philadelphia: Camino Books, 2007.

Dubin, Murray. *South Philadelphia: Mummers, Memories and the Melrose Diner*. Philadelphia: Temple University Press, 1996.

Elliott, Joseph E.B., Nathaniel Popkin, and Peter Woodall. *Philadelphia: Finding the Hidden City*. Philadelphia: Temple University Press, 2017.

Golden, Jane, Robin Rice, and Natalie Pompilio. *More Philadelphia Murals and the Stories They Tell*. Philadelphia, Temple University Press, 2006.

Hemphill, C. Dallett. *Philadelphia Stories: People and Their Places in Early America*. Philadelphia: University of Pennsylvania Press, 2021.

Kahan, Paul. *Philadelphia: A Narrative History*. Philadelphia: University of Pennsylvania Press, 2025

Kaufmann, Thomas. *Independence Bells of Philadelphia*. Charleston, SC: Arcadia Publishing, 2022

Lawson, Robert. *Ben and Me*. New York: Little, Brown Books, 1988.

Lester, Molly. *Building Ghosts: Past Lives and Lost Places in a Changing City*. Philadelphia: Temple University Press, 2024

Marion, John Francis. *Walking Tours of Historic Philadelphia*. Philadelphia: Institute for the Study of Human Issues, 1984.

Mauger, Ed. *Philadelphia in Photographs*. Bexley, OH: Gramercy Books, 2006.

Moss, Roger W. *Historic Landmarks of Philadelphia*. Philadelphia: University of Pennsylvania Press, 2008.

Murphy, Jim. *Real Philly History, Real Fast*. Philadelphia: Temple University, 2021

Nash, Gary. *First City Philadelphia and the Forging of Historical Memory*. Philadelphia: University of Pennsylvania Press, 2001.

Newman, Boyd and Linda. *Hikes Around Philadelphia*. Philadelphia: Temple University Press, 2011.

Pompilio, Natalie and Tricia Pompilio. *This Used to Be Philadelphia*. St. Louis: Reedy Press, 2021

Pompilio, Natalie and Tricia Pompilio. *Walking Philadelphia: 30 Walking Tours Featuring Art, Architecture, History and Little-Known Gems*. Birmingham, AL: Wilderness Press, 2022.

Web Sources

9th Street Italian Market: italianmarketphilly.org

African American Museum in Philadelphia: aamp.org

American Battlefield Trust: battlefields.org

American Heritage: americanheritage.com

American Philosophical Society: amphilsoc.org

The American Presidency Project at UC Santa Barbara: presidency.ucsb.edu

Americana Corner: americanacorner.com

Arch Street Meeting House: historicasmh.org

Archdiocese of Philadelphia: archphila.org

Association for Public Art: associationforpublicart.org

Billypenn at WHYY: billypenn.com

Carpenters Hall: carpentershall.org

Christ Church: christchurchphila.org

City of Philadelphia: phila.gov

The Constitutional Walking Tour: theconstitutional.com

Curbed Philly: philly.curbed.com

Descendants of the Signers of the Declaration of Independence: dsdi1776.com

Elfreth's Alley museum: elfrethsalley.org

Encyclopedia of Greater Philadelphia: philadelphiaencyclopedia.org

Famous 4th St. Delicatessen: famous4thstreetdelicatessen.com

Franklin Institute: fi.edu

Four Walls Whiskey: fourwallswhiskey.com

George Washington's Mount Vernon: mountvernon.org

Ghost City Tours: ghostcitytours.com

Global Philadelphia: globalphiladelphia.org

Gloria Dei (Old Swedes) Church: gloriadei.com

Greater Philadelphia Cultural Alliance: philaculture.org

Haunt Scout: hauntscout.com

Hidden City Philadelphia: hiddencityphila.org

Historic Philadelphia Inc: historicphiladelphia.org

The Historical Markets Database: hmdb.org

Historical Society of Pennsylvania: hsp.org

The History Channel: history.com

The Independence Hall Association: independenceassociation.org

The Independence Visitor Center: phlvisitorcenter.com

Instagram: instagram.com

Jewish Forward: forward.com

John F Kennedy Library Foundation: jfklibrary.org

Journal of the American Revolution: allthingsliberty.com

Junket: wejunket.com

Lest We Forget Slavery Museum: lwfsm.com

The Library Company of Philadelphia: Librarycompany.org

Library of Congress: Loc.gov

Locations of Lore: Locationsoflore.com

Mikveh Israel: mikvehisrael.org

Mother Bethel AME Church: motherbethel.org

Mural Arts Philadelphia: muralarts.org

Museum of the American Revolution: amrevmuseum.org

National Archives: archives.gov

The National Archives: blog.nationalarchives.gov.uk

National Archives/Founders Online: founders.archives.gov

National Constitution Center: constitutioncenter.org

National Liberty Museum: libertymuseum.org

Newspapers.com: newspapers.com

Old Pine Street Church: oldpine.org

Oxford Academic: academic.oup.com

PBS: pbs.org

Philadelphia magazine: phillymag.com

The Philadelphia Citizen: thephiladelphiacitizen.org

The *Philadelphia Inquirer*: inquirer.com

Philly History blog: blog.phillyhistory.org

Natalie Pompilio: nataliepompilio.com

National Catholic Register: ncregister.com

National Constitution Center: constitutioncenter.org

National Park Planner: npplan.com

National Park Service: nps.org

National Trust for Historic Preservation: savingplaces.org

National Underground Railroad Freedom Center: freedomcenter.org

Patch: patch.com

Pennsylvania Hospital: Ppnnmedicine.org

Penn Today: penntoday.upenn.edu

Philadelphia Convention and Visitors Bureau: discoverphl.com

The Philadelphia Contributionship: 1752.com

The Philadelphia Society for the Preservation of Landmarks: philalandmarks.org

The *Philadelphia Tribune*: phillytrib.com

Philadelphia Visitor Center Corp: phlvisitorcenter.com

Philly Voice: phillyvoice.com

Public Art Archive: publicartarchive.org

Queen Village Catholic: queenvillagecatholic.com

Ranker: ranker.com

Real Philly History with Jim Murphy: realphillyhistory.com

St. Peter's Church: stpetersphila.org

Smithsonian Institution: www.si.edu

South Street Headhouse Square District: southstreet.com

Spirits of '76 Ghost Tour: spiritsof76.com

SyFy network: syfy.com

Travelers Press: travelerspress.com

University of Washington: washington.edu

US Ghost Adventures: usghostadventures.com

US Office of the Historian: history.state.gov

UShistory.org: ushistory.org

Viator: viator.com

Visit Philadelphia: visitphilly.com

Washington Avenue Green: washingtonavenuegreen.com

The White House Historical Association: whitehousehistory.org

WHYY: whyy.org

Wikipedia: wikipedia.org

WorldAtlas: worldatlas.com

Weitzman National Museum of American Jewish History:tTheweitzman.org

Index

Eight F-8 squadrons made 13 deployments into the combat theater in *Essex*-class carriers during Rolling Thunder. In that time, one additional F-8 squadron made a single deployment in a *Midway*-class carrier and one Marine F-8 squadron in an *Essex*. To that number must be added many more RF-8G deployments as detachments to air wings in all carrier classes. As for battling North Vietnamese MiGs, the first full year of Rolling Thunder was disheartening: 5 MiGs downed in aerial combat for the loss of 3 F-8s, yielding no better than a 1.6-to-1 exchange rate. By the following year F-8 squadrons were finding their footing and adapting F-8 tactics so as to prevail over MiG tactics and performance. In 1967 9 MiGs were downed for no losses, a 9-to-0 exchange rate that approached the war-winning ratios of the latter days of World War II in the Pacific. Even with bombing limitations above the 19th Parallel beginning in April 1968 that made MiG appearances less frequent, F-8s achieved a still-respectable exchange rate, 5-to-0.

Not evident in the exchange rates were opportunities lost for shootdowns due to AIM-9s that "failed to guide" (whose guidance systems did not perform correctly due either to being launched out of the seeker's lock-on envelope or out of the missile's kinematic ability to negotiate very high g's, or as a result of damage to the missile suffered aboard ship in handling or loading) or to 20-mm guns that jammed. Both were on full display during events surrounding Hal Marr's MiG-17 shootdown of 12 June 1966. On that mission, four F-8s provided combat air patrol over an A-4 strike northwest of Haiphong, two from VF-211, piloted by Marr and Phil Vampatella, joined by two from VF-24, flown by Phil Richardson and Denis Duffy. Each F-8 was loaded with two AIM-9Ds and full loads of 20-mm ammunition; the flight of four orbited in a slow left turn at 2,500 feet and 400 knots. Four MiG-17s challenged them, and a head-on pass quickly devolved into individual engagements. Marr took down the first MiG with his second AIM-9D after the first missile failed to guide. He closed on another for a gun shot but realized both lower guns were inoperative due to an electrical system malfunction. He damaged a second MiG with 25 rounds from the operational guns before they jammed.

Vampatella tried an AIM-9D shot from his MiG's seven o'clock position at three quarters of a mile in a 4 g turn. With a good aural tone, he fired, but the missile never left the rail. He selected his second AIM-9D, which simply went ballistic. As another MiG flew through Vampatella's twelve o'clock, he tried a gun shot. His first eighty rounds missed; he closed to a thousand feet for a second attempt when his guns jammed after firing 100 rounds. Richardson's two AIM-9D shots failed to guide before he got off a hundred rounds of 20-mm with no effect, because his escaping target was getting farther away. Duffy, by this time recovered from back injuries sustained in his ramp-strike ejection nine months before (chapter 4), pressed his attack but was denied the shootdown: as he claimed later, "I would have had him if my guns worked." Overall, four F-8s fired eight AIM-9Ds with only one hit and fired 400 rounds of 20-mm with gun issues in all four.[1] The outcome of this melee could have been four MiGs destroyed instead of one for no losses had the weapons functioned properly and had they been employed properly.

THE F-8 FIGHTER WEAPONS SCHOOL

Concern over the lackluster performance of Navy weapons in Rolling Thunder prompted a comprehensive review in 1968 of missiles and training. Concern was heightened by recent controlled tests by VX-4 revealing that half of the shots were made "out of envelope." The Ault Report (for the study leader, Capt. Frank Ault) clearly pointed to the dismal experience with the AIM-7 Sparrow missile rather than the Sidewinder. To the extent that it underscored training inadequacies, it focused on F-4 aircrews and not on the F-8 community. The F-8 community had entered the conflict buoyed by its dogfighting ethos, but by the time of the Ault study, six of the ten fleet squadrons still operating the F-8 were due to decommission or transition to the F-4 within two years. The Crusader's days were clearly numbered, and most likely for that reason, the Ault Report did not review 20-mm gun reliability and employment issues. Yet there was considerable focus on the AIM-9, common to both F-4 and F-8, and on shortcomings in both F-4 and F-8 training for employment of the missile.

Section IV of the Ault Report dealt with aircrew training, readiness, doctrine, tactics, and procedures. The task leader for that section was Capt. Merle Gorder, who had been skipper of the first fleet Crusader squadron, VF-32, a decade before and subsequently a CO

of the F-8 FRS, VF-124. Among its recommendations was that F-8 pilots should carry out one actual AIM-9 shot in the FRS and two per year in the fleet thereafter. Furthermore, AIRPAC and AIRLANT (the type commanders, chapter 4) should standardize training and readiness manuals for fighters, with visual aids on AIM-9 systems. Section IV bemoaned the loss of expertise in fighter weaponry and doctrine with the decommissioning of FAGU in 1960 and accordingly rendered its most impactful recommendation: CNO and AIRPAC should establish an Advanced Fighter Weapons School in the Readiness Carrier Air Wing on the West Coast (RCVW-12) for both F-8 pilots and F-4 aircrews. After a successful trial period the formal training was to be expanded in the West Coast RAG and extended to the East Coast (RCVW-4).

Section IV noted that "concepts and plans for an Advanced Fighter Weapons School had already been formulated."[2] In fact, the F-8 Fighter Weapons School (FWS) opened its doors the first week of December 1968, a month ahead of the Ault Report's formal release, and a month before the F-4 "schoolhouse" opened under VF-121. CAG-12 (i.e., the CAG of CVW-12), Capt. Phil Craven, had got things off to a running start three months before even that, when he directed VF-124's CO, Cdr. Harry Post, to start up an advanced weapons training program. The working idea was to provide a higher level of air combat training in the F-8 than could be accomplished in a normal introductory VF-124 FRS syllabus—in other words, a postgraduate education in the employment of the F-8 and its entire weapons suite. F-8 squadron commanders nominated their most promising junior pilots to attend, each bringing with him a squadron aircraft to be paired against an instructor and aircraft from the FWS. The officer-in-charge of the F-8 FWS, Lt. Cdr. David Hellman, was joined by other combat-experienced F-8 pilots as instructors, including Lieutenant Commanders Richard Mudgett, Dave Morris, Larry Miller, and Ron Ball; Lieutenant Boyd Repsher, Bob Geeding, Bruce Johnson; and later Joe Phaneuf, Phil Wood, and Don Agatep.[3] Six junior officers made up the first FWS class, convening on 2 December 1968. The new students all had outstanding reputations in the community, and all knew each other.

Lt. Steve Marinshaw, a first-tour nugget with VF-162 aboard the USS *Ticonderoga* in 1969. Selected for the second of four classes assembled for "postgraduate" education in the F-8 and its employment, he joined a promising group of junior Crusader pilots who had shown excellent potential in their first squadron tours. (Steve Marinshaw)

Morning classroom instruction began in Hangar 2 at Miramar, with flying in the afternoons. The day concluded with four hours of study each evening. Classified briefings were conducted by the CVW-12 staff air intelligence officer on MiG performance and tactics, communist bloc air-to-air and ground-to-air weapons, and how to defeat them. Flight instruction began with one vs. one, progressed to one vs. two, then two vs. one, and finally two vs. two. FWS instructors dual-qualified in the A-4 and TA-4 flew as the "bogies" (hostiles) in Skyhawks made available by VF-126, the "adversary" squadron (opposition aircraft in training engagements, flying assessed enemy characteristics and tactics). The flight curriculum expanded to include bombing and strafing in the Chocolate Mountain Range and air-to-air gunnery in W-291 range offshore against a towed target.

The second of four FWS classes to convene included Lt. Steve Marinshaw from VF-162, who recalled his final FWS flight—a one vs. one against an F-4 from VF-121—as instructive:

> I orbited in W-291 [Warning Area 291 of the Southern California Range Complex] at 20,000' and only knew that a "bogie" was inbound from the east and I didn't know if he was high or low or what bearing he was from me. He had a very good radar and RIO [radar intercept officer, in the back seat] and I had none, so flew a north–south racetrack pattern while searching for him with binoculars. When I finally spotted him, he was at my 3 o'clock about 3,000 feet below me at about five miles heading towards my 6 o'clock, in zone 1 afterburner. Usually, you could spot an F4 at about 20 miles because of their smoke trails, but when in zone 1 A/B [close-range dogfighting in afterburner], they did not emit the characteristic smoke trail. He had much more kinetic energy than I did. I pulled a right turn into him at max g's in afterburner. He pulled a tighter climbing turn. The F-4 had a higher G-limit than the F8. I was in a defensive position and whatever I tried, I couldn't shake him and he eventually worked his F4 into a firing position on me. The F4 was an excellent dogfighter, especially when clean [i.e., aerodynamically, with minimal drag-producing fittings]. The pilot who humbled me was VF-121's Pete Pettigrew, a.k.a. "Mr. F-4."[4]

The F-8 FWS was phased out in the early 1970s after the fourth FWS class, as the sunset of active F-8 fleet squadrons—the withdrawal of F-8s from service—drew near.

HANDS-ON MIG EXPLOITATION

The F-8 Fighter Weapons School standup was bookended by two events that were at once eye-opening in themselves and closely aligned to the FWS curriculum. The first, code-named Project Have Doughnut, was a secret Defense Intelligence Agency program to evaluate the F-8 and other U.S. Navy and Air Force aircraft against an actual MiG-21. The second, sponsored by an Air Force command, the National Air and Space Intelligence Center, was known as Project Have Drill and pitted Air Force and Navy aircraft against an actual MiG-17. The MiG-21, acquired in a high-level exchange with Israel, was a MiG-21F-13, an export model of the kind seen in Rolling Thunder. When it arrived at Groom Lake in Nevada in early 1968 its qualities and limitations were wrung out in exploitation flights by Navy and Air Force pilots, to substantiate and supplement current intelligence data that was used in the FWS curriculum. Once the flying qualities were thoroughly understood, pilots in the MiGs flew maneuvers known to be commonly used by the original MiG operators, as witnessed in actual combat in North Vietnam. The results of the evaluation would contribute to the creation of the F-8 FWS and F-4 FWS as means to disseminate highly classified results to a broader set of service fighter pilots.

For the Navy, VX-4 members Tom Cassidy, Foster "Tooter" Teague, Ronald "Mugs" McKeown, and Mike Welch, participated—all lieutenant commanders and, as it happened, experienced F-8 pilots. Their flights against the MiG in F-8Es revealed the MiG-21 to be a worthy adversary in some flight regimes but also to have weaknesses in others could be exploited. The MiG-21 could out-accelerate the F-8 from a slow-speed start, but at high Mach the F-8 regained the advantage. In a turning contest at lower altitude, the MiG drained off energy (chapter 7) quicker but could retain the advantage in the turn, thanks to its very low "wing loading," the ratio of the aircraft's weight to the area of its wings, compared to the F-8. As the F-8 slowed in a turn, it would be at an increasing disadvantage. Below 16,000 feet the MiG-21 began to experience severe buffeting at 0.93 Mach, where the F-8 still had a considerable speed and maneuvering margin. The MiG's cockpit visibility was limited directly behind, allowing an F-8 to make an undetected low six o'clock approach for a missile shot. But if the closure continued, it was best to lag in the turn, pointing the nose to the outside of the turn radius, rather than lead within it. If the turn was matched and closure continued, the overtaking F-8 could pass the MiG and set itself up for an Atoll (Soviet-made IR-homing missile) shot. "Combat spread" patrolling—i.e., far enough apart for safety and maneuvering but close enough for mutual support—was determined to be still the most effective flight formation, especially for lookout, as the MiG proved very difficult to detect visually. Section "loose deuce" (sections of two aircraft about a mile apart), employed in Rolling Thunder, appeared to remain the best tactic against the MiG once engaged: one F-8 keeps the MiG occupied while the wingman maneuvers for the kill.[5]

In the spring of 1969, ten weeks after the first F-8 FWS class began, another exploitation event got under way in the high desert in the spring of 1969, this one with a MiG-17F also transferred to the United States by Israel. Navy members of the evaluation team found that although the MiG-17 (NATO code name Fresco) was not the performer that the MiG-21 had proved to be in the prior evaluation, it had attributes to be aware of and shortcomings to be exploited. F-8H and J models were flown against the MiG-17 in 16.5 missions (the "half" missions called off early for aircraft or range-clearance issues, given partial credit], and "every Navy pilot engaged in the project lost his first engagement with the Fresco C."[6] Overconfidence may have been involved, but other factors were certainly in play. Initially F-8 pilots found the MiG exceedingly difficult to see almost until radar observers saw the two contacts almost merge; soon thereafter they underestimated the MiG-17s sustained-turn capability with judicious use of afterburner below five hundred knots, largely a product of its very low wing loading compared to the F-8's. As learning progressed, the MiG-17's deficiencies of which the F-8 could take advantage became more apparent. F-8 pilots were advised when engaging MiG-17s to maintain a high energy advantage over the MiG's marginal control at high Q (chapter 2), keeping airspeed above 500 knots and definitely avoiding high-g maneuvers below 500 knots. The F-8 had the advantage in thrust-to-weight ratio, which equated to much more robust climb performance—the lesson being to draw the MiG-17 into the vertical whenever possible. Finally, mutual support with a wingman was judged an absolute necessity. MiG exploitation and FWS training kept the fires burning in the F-8 community, such that when intensive bombing restarted in Vietnam, the edge was still sharp. The transition to the F-4 was nearly complete, but four squadrons were left for Southeast Asia deployment.

F-8E vs. MiG-21F

Performance Measure	F-8E
ACCELERATION	
CRT Power < 1.0 M	F-8 = Faster A/B Light-Off MiG-21 Catches Up
CRT Power > 1.1 M	
DECELERATION	
Level *G*	More Effective Speed Brake
High *G*	Lower Energy Loss Rate
ROLL RATE	
*Max *Q**	MiG: Severe Buffer at .93 M
*SUSTAINED *G* < 16,000'*	
above 450 KIAS	
below 450 KIAS	
ZOOM (CRT ≤ 36,000')	Slight Disadvantage

Advantage | Comparable | Disadvantage

Source: "Project Have Doughnut - Tactical Report", Vol. II, 1 August 1969 declassified IAW 12958, 23 Mar 2000, Defense Intelligence Agency

Performance comparison of the F-8 vs. MiG-21F-13. A MiG-21 captured by Israel was transferred to the Defense Intelligence Agency for evaluation in 1968 at Groom Lake. Flown against several types of Navy and Air Force aircraft; against the F-8, the MiG was evaluated in one-on-one and two-on-one offensive and defensive tactics. Results confirmed, and also revealed, MiG-21 deficiencies that could be exploited by the F-8. (National Air and Space Intelligence Center)

F-8E vs. MiG-17F

Performance Measure	F-8E
ACCELERATION	
MRT Power	Significantly Superior
CRT Power	Significantly Superior
DECELERATION	
Level *G*	
High *G*	
ROLL RATE	
*Max *Q**	Significantly Superior
*SUSTAINED *G* < 16,000'*	
above 450 KIAS	
below 450 KIAS	
ZOOM (CRT ≤ 36,000')	Significantly Superior

Advantage | Comparable | Disadvantage

Source: "Project Have Drill/Have Ferry - Tactical Report", Vol. II April 1970 declassified IAW 12958, 3 Oct 1997 National Air and Space Intelligence Center

Performance comparison of Crusader vs. MiG-17F. Controlled in-flight comparisons were conducted in 1969 by members of VX-4 flying F-8J/Hs against captured MiG-17Fs in exploitation flights known as Have Drill/Have Ferry. Navy pilots flew the F-8 in 16.5 one-on-one and two-on-two evaluations. Key takeaways: maintain high energy (500–600 knots airspeed), draw the fight into the vertical when possible, and engage only as a section, with strict mutual support. (DIA)

OPERATION LINEBACKER

North Vietnamese divisions rushed across the Demilitarized Zone separating North and South at the 17th Parallel on the last weekend of March 1972. A stepped-up response from Navy air wings offshore began to stem the onslaught and prevent the collapse of South Vietnamese ground forces. The resumption of intensive Navy bombing of North Vietnamese infrastructure began on 10 May with Operation Linebacker. From the USS *Hancock*, soon joined by the USS *Oriskany*, Air Wings 19 and 21, respectively, put all four F-8 squadrons on the line at Yankee Station to provide cover for restarted alpha strikes. But F-4 squadrons from the *Coral Sea* and *Kitty Hawk* air wings, soon joined by those from the *Constellation*, *Midway*, *America*, and *Saratoga* more often drew the fighter escort role. Fewer F-8 missions over the interior of North Vietnam usually meant that F-4s were more often in position to sight and engage the MiGs that came up.

In one last MiG engagement, though, the F-8's fearsome reputation among the enemy was recorded for posterity, even if unofficially. A section of VF-211 F-8Js from the *Hancock* were orbiting over the target as combat air patrol for an air-wing-strength strike coming off a target near Vinh. The F-4s of a section of strike-group escorts had lost sight of each other. Red Crown (the radar control ship offshore, chapter 7) vectored the F-4s away and vectored in the F-8s onto a lone MiG-17 flying in low from the coast. Lt. Cdr. Frank Bachman was in the lead, Lt. (jg) Jerry Tucker flying wing. Bachman was unable to see the MiG even when their tracks merged on the controller's radar. Then Tucker caught a glint of sunlight off the MiG's canopy, well below them. Tucker called tally ho (target in sight), but when his leader still couldn't see him, Tucker guided the section to a rear-quarter intercept. Completing a descending left turn to line up for the Sidewinder shot, Tucker was about to take it when he was more than a little startled to see the MiG pitch downward and a white parachute blossom in its wake. The MiG pilot ejected before either he or the F-8 had fired a shot. Much speculation has surrounded this "shootdown." By any measure this was not aggressive behavior on the part of the MiG pilot; maybe he had been told not to engage by his ground controllers. In any case, Lieutenant (junior grade) Tucker was never given official credit for the destroyed MiG.

GUNFIGHTER SUNSET

The days of gunfighter F-8s were waning by the mid-1970s, reduced in numbers either by squadron decommissionings or replacement by the F-4 Phantom. The Marine Corps had completed its transition out of the fighter F-8s before the end of the 1960s. Aside from the four fleet squadrons, Gunfighter Crusaders flew on with a few fleet composite (mixed-type) squadrons and two NAS Dallas reserve squadrons until 1975, when retirement began for them all. The last fleet squadrons to step out of the gunfighter were VF-191 and VF-194 in 1976.

The photo reconnaissance RF-8G flew on with VFP-63 until 1982, when the "sword was passed" to the two reserve squadrons still flying the RF-8G, VFP-206 and -306. It was a real sword, a recognizable token

Vought test pilot John Konrad delivers the XF8U-1 to the Vice Chief of Naval Operations, Adm. James Russell, on 25 October 1960, after 67 months of testing that included 508 flights. Admiral Russell had been a named recipient on behalf of the Navy of the 1956 Collier Trophy awarded the F-8. Konrad had represented Charles McCarthy, senior Vought executive, corecipient of the Collier on behalf of the Vought Aircraft Company. The Navy donated the aircraft to the Smithsonian National Air and Space Museum for storage at Silver Hill, Maryland, before restoration. (NHHC)

of the Crusader community. In 1967 Lt. Cdr. Bruce Moorhouse, an instructor in VF-124 dissatisfied with the lack of a suitable community mascot, went to an antique weapons dealer and purchased an authentic 13th-century sword, supposedly used by a crusader of that period. When VFP-63 took on the instruction of all new Crusader pilots, it inherited the sword. VFP-63 was the last active-duty fleet Crusader squadron, and in 1982 its last two RF-8Gs were flown to the desert "boneyard," by its commanding officer, Cdr. David Beam, and executive officer, Cdr. Grover "Skip" Giles. Reserve squadron VFP-306 was disestablished only two years later, leaving VFP-206 at Naval Air Facility Washington (at what was then Andrews Air Force Base) as the last remaining U.S. Navy Crusader squadron until it followed in 1987.[7]

Shortly after 9:30 a.m. on 30 March of that year, Cdr. Dave Strong, CO of VFP-206, performed a preflight inspection of his RF-8G and, other squadron members watching, shook hands with his plane captain and climbed into the cockpit for the last flight of a U.S. Navy Crusader. It was a short, twenty-minute hop to the Washington Dulles International Airport for delivery to storage and later display at the Smithsonian National Air and Space Museum. The day before, a formal ceremony in Washington, D.C., occasioned the disestablishment of VFP-206. It was attended by over seven hundred guests, including John Konrad, the Vought test pilot who had flown the very first experimental prototype thirty-two years before and in 1960 delivered that XF8U-1 to Washington. The XF8U-1 was received for donation to the Smithsonian Air and Space Museum by Adm. James Russell, Vice CNO, former chief of BuAer and recipient of the Collier Trophy for the Crusader's design and development. At the 206 ceremony the restored XF8U-1 and the retiring RF-8G were parked nose to nose as a fitting backdrop and tribute.[8]

THE NASA MISSIONS

The F-8 had been serving the nation in an entirely different way, as a testbed for two high-profile NASA programs. In the first, two F-8s were sent in the early

Project test pilot for the Digital Fly-by-Wire program, Gary Krier, made the first flight in May 1972. Krier was later Director of Flight Operations at the NASA Dryden Flight Research Center, Edwards, California. (NASA)

SCW Project test pilot Tom McMurtry stands in front of the highly modified F-8A that he flew for the first SCW test in March 1971. McMurtry would go on to become Associate Director for Flight Operations at NASA Dryden Flight Research Center at Edwards. (NASA)

A Vought F-8C reconfigured with computer-controlled, fiber-optic-relayed flight control actuation as the centerpiece of NASA's Digital Fly-By-Wire program. (NASA)

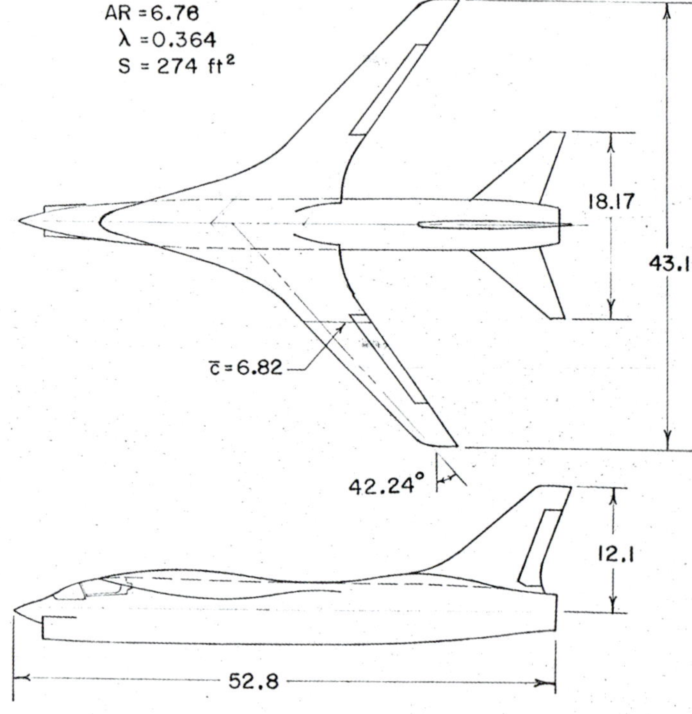

NASA's Dr. Richard Whitcomb, chief of transonic aerodynamics at Langley Research Center, conceived a supercritical-wing shape that provided higher lift-to-drag ratios at the same speeds by using thicker airfoil sections and reducing wing sweepback. The F-8 proved the ideal candidate for testing the Supercritical Wing. Initial drawings gave the familiar Crusader a radically new profile. (National Air and Space Museum)

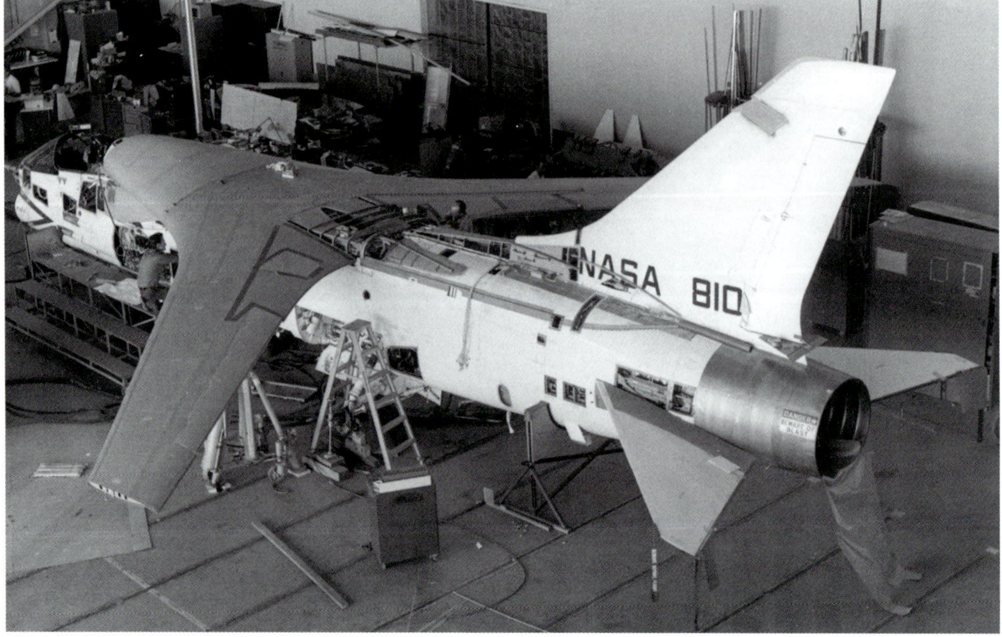

The Vought F-8A had the advantage of Mach speed and an easily removable wing that was modified with the new Supercritical Airfoil, provided by North American Aviation. (National Air and Space Museum)

1970s to NASA to support its Digital Fly-by-Wire program: a TF-8A served as the proficiency vehicle for NASA test pilots, and an F-8C was remade to swap out numerous, failure-prone flight-control mechanical linkages and push rods for that a computer system that received pilot stick inputs and transmitted those over fiber-optic wire to actuators. The first of 210 flights was conducted in May 1972. The results were improved reliability, less weight, and less space. The payoff for NASA was carryover of the technology validated on the F-8C to the Lunar Landing Training Vehicle, which prepared the Apollo astronauts for the moon landing, and ultimately to the Space Shuttle itself. The pay-off for the flying public was the incorporation of digital fly-by-wire into most modern airliners, beginning with the Airbus 320 in 1987, followed by Boeing's 777 in 1994.

The F-8 supercritical wing project flew from 1971 to 1973 and amassed 86 flights. Analysis confirmed that it increased transonic efficiency of the F-8 by as much as 15 percent. (ALAMY)

The second contribution to NASA was related to its Supercritical Wing. At the Langley Research Center in the early 1960s Dr. Richard Whitcomb, chief of the Transonic Aerodynamics Branch, had done the exploratory research and patented the concept. NASA selected an F-8A as the testbed for a practical demonstration of Whitcomb's airfoil at the Dryden Flight Research Center (chapter 5). Rockwell's North American Aircraft Division built the wing, which was mounted on the F-8 and flight-tested between 1971 and 1973. Tests showed that the wing increased the F-8's efficiency in the transonic region by as much as 15 percent. Boeing adopted the technology for its 787, using it to save 20 percent on fuel usage by lowering speed from transonic to high subsonic.

THE LAST CRUSADERS

Encroachment on the territorial claims of the Philippine government in the Spratly Islands by the People's Republic of China was motivation enough for the Philippine air force (PAF) to consider a purchase of F-8Hs. Late-model Crusaders were reclaimed from desert storage in Arizona; twenty-five were refurbished and ten bought as spares, all for $11.7 million in 1977. For another $23 million, eighteen pilots from the Philippine air force and PAF maintainers were given transition training at Vought in Grand Prairie. Deliveries were completed by 1979; the airplanes served for ten years before the PAF was reduced to eight mission-capable airplanes. Funding was simply unavailable to support maintainer training, spares, and the fuel usage required for proficiency. The PAF decommissioned its remaining F-8Hs in 1988, offering them for sale as scrap in 1991.

The French navy had more success with its F-8E(FNs. Two squadrons, 12F and 14F, under Carrier Air Wing 2, stood up with their Crusaders, alternating deployments in the *Clemenceau* and *Foch* as the situation dictated. Squadron 14F transitioned out of its Crusaders in 1979, taking on a strike role with newly delivered Super Étendards. Squadron 12F continued on as the sole Crusader squadron maintained by the French naval air arm. By 1989, after withdrawing from the European study group that fostered development of the Typhoon fighter, it undertook to develop an indigenous design, the Rafale fighter. The Rafale carrier-based variant would not be available for nearly ten years, so the French put their F-8E(FN)s through renovation to span the gap until the Rafale-M could be available. The renovated F-8E(FN) became the F-8P, for Prolongé, in reference to its extended life. Key updates included new electric wiring, an instrument landing system, a new inertial navigation system, and new Martin-Baker Mk 7 ejection seats to replace the older Mk F5s. The F-8Ps of 12.F Squadron, in their last extended deployment,

Upon the retirement of the last operational F-8 squadron, a F-8E(FN) of Flotille 12F based at Landivisiau, Brittany, makes a fly-by for American and French Crusader pilots gathered for the ceremony. (ALAMY)

aboard *Foch* in March 1999, flew day and night in support of bombing raids over Kosovo. Once the deployment was over, the squadron began downsizing.

A ceremony in France on 3 December 1999 brought down the curtain on the Crusader's active military service anywhere. Members of the French l'Aeronautique Navale, which had last experienced the F-8, were true advocates for their aircraft and retired it with not a little somber melancholy. But they marked the occasion with a send-off worthy of the Crusader's forty-four years of service in the liveries of the U.S. Navy, U.S. Marine Corps, French navy, and Philippine air force. Four F-8Ps performed an abbreviated air show that bent the rules on speed and altitude. This was followed by a banquet the next night at the Chateau Brezal, a country estate belonging to the commander of the Aeronavale. In attendance was the first French navy pilot to train in the F-8, at VF-174 in 1964, Yves Goupil, and the last squadron commander, who had flown lead in the send-off air show, Capitaine de frégate Antoine Guillot. Hundreds of Americans attended from Vought and from the U.S. Navy and Marine Corps, some from VF-154, the first West Coast squadron to fly the Crusader, in 1957. One veteran Navy Crusader pilot recalled the weekend celebration: Both French and American, Navy and Marine [F-8 pilots attended]. Guys with everything from 300 to 3,000 hours in the F-8; some who just flew it, most who deeply loved it—with a passion perhaps surpassing any other love in our lives. The French pilots from the last active squadron were wonderful. And they flew the plane beautifully and illegally. The airshow passes were often at less than 100 feet, and more than 500 knots, all right over us. Oil cooler doors open, hard lights on the burners passing over our heads; the noise too powerful to be heard, only felt. Glorious! Yves, French F-8 pilot No. 1, and [now] a retired French admiral, spontaneously climbed up onto a chair on the stage, and in highly accented English said: "When I went to VF 174 to learn the F-8, they taught me one most important thing: When you are out of F-8's, you are out of fighters!" The place went crazy, as you might expect.[9]

NOTES

1. John S. Attinelio, Project Leader, Southeast Asia: Account of F-4 and F-8 Events Prior to 1 March 1967," Institute for Defense Analyses, Systems Evaluation Division, October 1967, 223–25.

2. Frank Ault, Capt., USN, "Report of the Air-to-Air Missile System Capability Review," Naval Air Systems Command, July–November 1968, 37, accessed 19 July 2024, https://apps.dtic.mil/sti/tr/pdf/ADA955143., 37.

3. Chance Vought Aircraft, "First Class Completes 'Post Grad Course.'" (LTV Aerospace Corporation, Dallas, TX) *Crusader Fighter Report* 3, no. 2. (February 1969), http://f8crusader.org/LTV_CFR/LTV%20Crusader%20Fighter%20Report%201969%20Vol.%203.pdf.

4. Marinshaw interview, 15 July 2024.

5. Ault.

6. Thomas R. Woodford, "Project Have Drill/Have Ferry Tactical Evaluation," National Air and Space Intelligence Center, April 1970, accessed 19 July 2024 at https://nsarchive2.gwu.edu/NSAEBB/NSAEBB443/docs/area51_51.PDF.

7. Robert Frantz, Lt., USN, "VFP-63 Passes the Sword," *Naval Aviation News* (November 1982), 40, https://www.history.navy.mil/research/histories/.

8. Cdr. Peter Mersky, USN (Ret.), "The Last Launch" *Naval Aviation News* (July/August 1987), 18–20, https://www.history.navy.mil/research/histories/.

9. Larry Nowak, "Gator Tales," *F-8 Crusader Association*, http://f8crusader.org/gatrtalz.htm.

BIBLIOGRAPHY

Air Force Systems Command, Foreign Technology Division. *Have Doughnut: Tactical*. DIA Task T65-20-2. Defense Intelligence Agency, 1 August 1969.

Arbiter, Jerry "Biter," Commander, USN (Ret.). Interview by Ernest Snowden, 7 July 2024.

Attinelio, John S., Project Leader. "Air-to-Air Encounters in Southeast Asia: Account of F-4 and F-8 Events Prior to 1 March 1967." Institute for Defense Analyses, Systems Evaluation Division, October 1967.

Ault, Frank, Captain, USN. "Report of the Air-to-Air Missile System Capability Review." Naval Air Systems Command, July–November 1968, accessed 19 July 2024, https://apps.dtic.mil/sti/tr/pdf/ADA955143.pdf.

Bernier, Robert. "Forty Years Building a Dream." *Air and Space Quarterly*, 21 September 2022.

Burtenshaw, Edward C., Colonel, USAF. "Project Current Historical Evaluation of Counterinsurgency Operations (CHECO)." Hickam AFB, HI: PACAF, 8 March 1966, accessed 10 June 2024, https://apps.dtic.mil/sti/pdfs/ADA486857.pdf.

Butler, Tony. *Early US Jet Fighters: Proposals, Projects and Prototypes*. Hikoki, 2013.

Central Intelligence Agency, Intelligence Directorate. "MiG-21F-13 Aircraft Manual," June 1963, accessed 15 June 2024 at https://www.cia.gov/readingroom/docs/CIA-RDP80T00246A030700180001-1.pdf.

———. "Sources of Military Equipment to Viet Cong and North Vietnamese Military Forces," 4 November 1968, accessed 15 June 2024 at https://www.cia.gov/readingroom/docs/DOC_0000381439.pdf.

———. "Summary of Civilian Damage in Hanoi," 29 May 1967, accessed 6 July 2024 at https://www.cia.gov/readingroom/docs/CIA-RDP78S02149R000200080003-8.pdf.

Campbell, Douglas E. *Flight, Camera, Action*. Syneca Research, 2014.

Chance Vought Aircraft. "F8U-1P Detail Specification, SD-500-1-1," August 1955. National Archives and Records Administration, College Park, MD.

"Chance Vought F8 Crusader." Flight Safety Foundation, *Flight Safety Network*, accessed 19 July 2024 at https://asn.flightsafety.org/wikibase/type/F8/4.

———. "XF8U-1 Program History," 1958. Vought Aircraft Company Collection, University of Texas at Dallas.

Charyk, Joseph V., Director NRO. "Interdepartmental Cover Support to Operation Blue Moon." National Reconnaissance Office, accessed 15 June 2024, http://www.cia.gov/readingroom/docs/.

Combs, Thomas, S., Rear Admiral, USN. BuAer Letter Aer-CT-3 (191400), 18 May 1953, National Archives and Records Administration, Record Group 72, Box 404, College Park, MD.

Connors, Jack. *The Engines of Pratt & Whitney: A Technical History*. American Institute of Aeronautics and Astronautics, 2010.

Davies, Peter. *F-8 Crusader: Vietnam 1963–1973*. Osprey, 2023.

———. *F-4 Phantom II vs. MiG-21*. Osprey, 2008.

Dobbs, Michael. "The Photographs That Prevented World War III." *Smithsonian Magazine*, October 2012, accessed 15 June 2024, https://www.smithsonianmag.com/history/the-photographs-that-prevented-world-war-iii-36910430/.

Dorr, Robert F. "F8U-3 Crusader Was Really Hot Might Have Been." *Defense Media Network*, 17 November 2012, accessed 19 July 2024, https://www.defensemedianetwork.com/stories/f8u-3-crusader-was-really-hot-might-have-been/.

Dosé, Curt, Commander, USN (Ret.). Interview by Ernest Snowden, 10 June 2024.

Elward, Brad. "The Navy's 'Other' Fighter Weapons School." (Tailhook Association) *Hook Magazine* 49, no. 1,. San Diego, CA (Spring 2021).

Elward, Brad. *TOPGUN: The Legacy*. Schiffer Military, 2021.

Engen, Donald D., Vice Admiral, USN (Ret.). *Wings and Warriors: My Life as a Naval Aviator*. Smithsonian Institution Press, 1997.

Evans, Mark L., and Roy A. Grossnick. *United States Naval Aviation 1910–2010*. Naval History and Heritage Command, 2015, repr. Uncommon Valor, 2016.

Francillon, René. *Grumman Aircraft*. Naval Institute Press, 1989.

Frantz, Robert, Lieutenant, USN. "VFP-63 Passes the Sword." *Naval Aviation News* (November 1982), https://www.history.navy.mil/research/histories/.

"Gator Tales." *F-8 Crusader Association*. accessed July 2024 at http://f8crusader.org/gatrtalz.htm.

Gillcrist, Paul T., Rear Admiral, USN (Ret.). *Crusader! Last of the Gunfighters*. Schiffer Military, 1995.

Glenn, John, Colonel, USMC (Ret.), with Nick Taylor. *John Glenn: A Memoir*. Bantam, 1999.

Gundlach, Louis. "The Last of the Gunfighter: F-8 Crusader over North Vietnam." *Hush Kit*, 6 September 2020, accessed May 2024 at https:/hushkit.net/2020/09/06/the-last-gunfighter-analysis-of-f-8-crusader-success-over-north-vietnam.